# Surviving Foster Care
# And
# Making It Work
# For You!

I0429309

# Tanya Cooper

ISBN-13:978-1461039730
ISBN-10:1461039738

# DEDICATION

This book is dedicated to Lisa Steinberg, a girl who was abused and beaten to death by her adoptive lawyer dad. To the kids who were burned in the oven and the boys drowned by their own mother. (Those reading and in pain must remember: you are here, they are not. Doesn't that mean anything to you? Why did God or the universe spare your life?

To M.R, one of ten children, who in the end could not beat a heroin addiction or her love for Jack Danielle's. M.R. fell so deeply into addiction that she eventually had to abandon her four children.

To my girls Arielle and Tatiana: without you life would have been less of an adventure. Thanks for taking me on many journeys but the best has been the journey of unconditional love.

This book would be impossible without the one lady who took a chance on my brother and me when no one else would take two siblings. M.W., in spite of what happened, you taught me style, class and that a good education could get a person far.

My only dad because I never knew my birth father, thanks J.D; you were the best dad a girl could have after seven years old, and thanks for believing me.

In spite of what happened, I received the two most important things a survivor of abandonment and abuse needs – love and structure.

This book is also dedicated to my brother Robert, who has since passed. You are always the inspiration for my heart beating. I will miss you and I will keep your memory alive by helping foster children reach their full potential.

To my brother Mark, I have not seen you since you were adopted by another family in Elmsford, New York, but know that I look for you every day and will not feel complete until I find you and know you are safe and loved.

To my birth sister, call her T, it is not our fault they separated us, thanks for the sacrifices you made as a child, I love you, and you are my hero.

Norma & Brown, "Baka", thanks for treating me like your own.

Reg and Anthony, thanks for all of your support & friendship.

To Gamilah, a counselor who believed in me and taught me to "Rise to the occasion and never let them see you sweat!" I learned to dismantle all of my anger and put it into writing. You knew I had a gift, and you helped me focus on the gift not the anger.

One counselor, teacher, or friend can make a difference!

To Gamilah's mother, the late, great Dr. Betty Shabazz, you were a true superwoman and an inspiration, a beacon of light when I was blinded.

I remember meeting you as a teen, seeing the look of potential and expectation in your eyes.

Your encouraging smile meant the world to me! By that smile and your voice, by your overall stature I knew it was time to rise and shine and take responsibility for my life!

When I meet a great person I often wonder who their parents are. When I met you, I knew why your daughter was so giving and patient, a counselor of change. Thanks for birthing someone who in turn saved my life.

Thanks to your family, for letting me sit in the circle, not out. It is so important for a foster child to meet other people's families; it is more important that those family members are receptive and accepting. You were my role models, thanks it made a difference in how I viewed women and what role I wanted to play in this life – strong, positive, leading, loving woman.

Sister L.M , God rest your soul, when I had no where to go after the abuse in foster care, you and the nuns took me in and taught me how to live after trauma. Thanks to you and the sisters for getting the healing ball rolling. When I went off to Paris the first time, you gave me numbers so I could feel comfortable in another country, and when I was homeless you took a chance and helped me back on my feet.

Thanks for taking the risk on me, it made me not give up and taught me the importance of helping others. I also learned, at what I thought was my lowest point, that there are angels right here on earth! St. Helena's - you gave me a new life!

At my second foster home in Westchester, I had great friends and neighbors. They were so good to me I often forgot I was a foster child. Neighbors do matter and everyone is vital in a foster child's growth!

DJ, R.T, and PL, CL, you were my confidants when I was hurting the most and could not tell a soul. By going to your homes I was allowed to escape abuse temporally and your families showed me love I never received in the group homes.

To the late Mr. Hammid, my favorite teacher for believing in me, because of you I have learned to never stop teaching and reaching one. Without us the world would be cold.

# ACKNOWLEDMENTS

Robert
Jackie Lethem
Bobby
Elizabeth
Arielle
Tatiana
Norma
Nancy
Brown
Megan
Adam
Ms. Summerford

Thank you for helping me move forward.
There are times when we encounter people who ask: what
are you doing, there are also times when you meet people
like you all who ask: how can I be of service, for this I
thank you all.

# Preface

This book is based on my experiences growing up in foster care from the ages of five to twenty-one and on my travels in the United States and Europe.

I learned to travel from my second foster mother, from the time she took Rob and me, until the day I left her home. She would often take Rob and me on her trips to the South, were she would often be the guest preacher for Sunday.

Traveling from New York to the South can be quite a trip for a seven year old. I would notice when we were in a "Nice" place and when we were in a "not so nice place." as I got older, I knew when I was in "the hood" or the Suburbs just by the houses, apartments or buildings and by the way people dressed and carried themselves. This travel bug would follow me out of foster care.

When I started modeling and went to stay in Paris, I made it a rule: always go to the "hood", which will let you know how people are really living. I also learned to stop at the nearest orphanage because that too will tell you how the people in a region, state, or city feel about the less fortunate.

I must say New York has a good track record of taking care of their homeless and less fortunate. New York also spends a lot of money trying to make those children in foster care feel special. Yes, there are always flaws in any system but I am not writing to focus on flaws; while I may mention a few, my main goal is for our children in foster care to walk away from the system feeling empowered and able to grow to their fullest potential, without remorse. I want each kid to point the finger at him or herself and say I am responsible for my future.

# CONTENTS

## Forward

I survived sixteen years of foster care. During that time I experienced sexual abuse and forced separation from an older sister and younger brother.

After talking with hundreds of children now in foster care as well as adults who aged out, I had what Oprah calls an Aha Moment.

Where, I wondered, was the book from our perspective? The book that told kids all the things I know now that I wished I had known back then.

This is that book. I share it so that others can learn what I didn't learn until I was thirty (missing out on so much life has to offer): you are worthwhile.

You have a right to a safe and happy life. If you are sexually or physically abused, you can still rise and be the best you.

Those horrible acts happened to you and may even define you BUT they are not the "only" thing that happened to you.

There is higher purpose and real good in your life. To survive and even thrive, you must find them.

If you happen to read this as an adult survivor, that's OK. You will now have a witness to your story and can learn how to put it all away and move on to greatness.

If you are a provider, you can gain insight and hopefully use it to help at least one child reach their full potential.

In the United States their are approximately 500,000 kids in foster care in America, about 30,000 foster children a year "age out" of the system.

Aging out means the individual comes of age and is now responsible for him or herself. This happens, depending on the state, at age eighteen or twenty-one.

At that time, the foster child is "freed" from the State agency they were placed with. Yes, they are "legally freed." In basic terms, the agency separates, signs off on all paperwork, saying you are no longer theirs to take care of financially, physically or mentally.

You are sent out into the cold world with no parents, no one to help you and, usually, no plan for the future. Imagine leaving an institution with no family, money, plan or support?

And thousands of these young people were sexually and physically abused while at home and/or in foster care. Why are we surprised when many are later found in jail, homeless or on drugs?

Over 30,000 young lives every year are at risk. We must encourage them before they leave the system rather than incarcerate them after they leave. Who is responsible?

All who pay taxes pay in the end because it is our money funding the prisons, halfway houses, rehabilitation programs, treatment centers and medication. To this list we should add education, intervention and information; these are key to foster children surviving the system and becoming the best person they can be.

New laws are in the works that would provide support for everyone in foster care through to age twenty-one. These laws are needed, but at whatever age people age out they will need some basic survival tools, such as planning skills, as well as a foundation of self worth.

A child who grows into a criminal may have never learned how to love and respect him or herself. Someone, or many someones, said the wrong things, did the wrong things, or did not say or do anything.

We are our brother's keepers, and our sister's.

Please note that most of those involved in foster care do an excellent job. The system has come a long way from when I struggled within it in the 70's. Yet I just know from surveying hundred of kids, it needs improvement.

Their needs to be a focus on self love and they should learn about energy and positive thinking, as taught in DVD's like Secret, (by Rhonda Byrne). Reading books like: The Art of happiness by The Dali Lama . . The goal should be to change the mind to postive dreamers who are are not afraid to achieve greatness. The intention of this book is to help those who already went through the system gain understanding and clarity and help those that are in the system currently get the mental tools they need to survive before aging out.

# 1
## Tanya's Version of Brooklyn History 101 - Why Would a Woman Give up her Four Children?

I was born in the heart of Brooklyn at a time when black was beautiful and afro's were in. Black was all around me and as a kid it was all good because no one was complaining for a kid to hear.

My older sister T. made me feel that I was indeed beautiful and special. Up until the age of five I had her, my mother, my baby brother's Mark and Rob. A struggling family of five.

Around August 27, 1971, the four children were taken into state custody. Because he was still an infant, Mark would soon be placed with a doctor's family in Elmsford, New York. For a time, the rest of us would have weekly visits with him.

When I first saw the group home where they put the rest of us, I could not figure out why I was with these kids running all over a campus or who these adults were, asking so many questions.

No one bothered to explain much back in 1971, especially to a kid.

When it comes to why my mother gave up her rights to her four children, it is important to understand the atmosphere in Brooklyn during the early 1960's. Thanks to Rosa Parks, we could sit anywhere on the bus, but a woman, much less a black woman with kids and barely a high school education, had few options for work.

The Vietnam War was taking our best men while at home assassins had gunned down first President Kennedy, then Dr. King and finally Malcolm X. Despair was the look I most often saw on the faces of adults, sadness and defeat the prevailing mood of the neighborhood. I've spoken with others who lived through these times in Brooklyn and similar cities and they remember the same despair. It was a mood that made fertile ground for the heroin that followed so many veterans home from Vietnam.

We know more know about post-traumatic-stress disorder, and we do more for veterans and family's now, but back then, with that unpopular war, they were on their own.

As I grew from a toddler to a small child, addiction rates grew too. My mother, then a young woman, was married to a man she had met through her brother.

They had one baby girl, named T. Then he was drafted, and while he was away, things began to go wrong. Maybe the drugs replaced him, numbed the loneliness.

I don't know. I do know she had me and then two more children, all of us by different men. She fell ever deeper into heroin addiction and was soon neglecting us.

What is my memory of those early years?

You may be surprised to hear that I believed it was all OK, because my siblings were with me. We got through things together. Once we were separated though, I was lost.

My mom was out on another drug binge and we had not seen her in weeks. We were hungry, yes, we were severely neglected, but we were home and we had each other.

My sister T. looked upset.

Only eight years old, she carried the burden of wondering how she was going to feed us.

She knew kids should be eating and getting fresh air. She must have heard us say we were hungry a hundred times that day. Somehow she got some butter and sugar and we ate it as if it was steak.

I did not know until years later that T. was the one who called Child Protective Services (CPS). She was tired, she could no longer watch us starve.

I know it broke her heart to make that call, but I know now – despite all that would happen to to us – she did the right thing.

After that day, we had food and shelter, but we also began to experience chaos, separation and mental neglect. We became "Wards of the court," Nobody's kids", "Foster kids". My friend Pat calls it "Legally kidnapped."

I am grateful for being taken out of a neglected home. I was able to flourish. I am not blaming anyone nor do I hold any animosity toward anyone.

The abuse I was to sustain in my second foster home would be outweighed by the good that also happened in that home. And had I never had these experiences, good and bad, I would not be the outspoken advocate for foster children that I am.

I am grateful for my life. I could have been aborted or killed. I wasn't.

I am here to speak what I know. I begin with a small child's memories.

## 2

## Crossing the Brooklyn Bridge -
## Separation and Abuse

A child is being taken away from her home in the middle of the night. Maybe it's early in the morning after the sun has risen and mother still has not made it home.

The knock at the door hasn't come yet. The child is playing make believe school with her siblings, because there are no toys. A couple of younger ones are crying because there's nothing to eat and mom's been gone for weeks.

Then the knock comes. It's a policeman and a social worker (in the 1970's that would usually have been a woman in a polyester suit, long hair, maybe a hippie dressed up). With no warning, the children are taken away from everything familiar.

This happened to me. Maybe it happened to you. I was too young to know my mom was nodding out from heroin, that she had fallen in love with Jack Daniels. And I was too innocent to realize I was being neglected, starved, mistreated, mis-educated and most importantly, set up to be ripped from the only family I had ever known.

## Alien Invasion

I wake one day hungry as usual but for some reason happy. While I'm playing and running through our empty two bedroom apartment, we hear a knock on the door. My sister answers and says, "it is the police". The next thing you know, we are told to come with these aliens and bring our suitcase. But we don't have a suitcase, so we put your things in a plastic bag one of them gives us and we go. I don't turn for a last look at our first home. We have no idea We'll never see it again.

None of us has ever been in a car before. Through its windows the city changes fast . . . bigger buildings, better dressed people, and in all colors, speaking English we have not heard in our ears or spoken out of our mouths.

The aliens take us to unknown places in Brooklyn, we stay for a while. We later go again to a place that we find out is called Manhattan. We are thinking, "Where is our mother, who are these people, are they people?" They treat us like we are a rare animal meant for the zoo. They talk to us like we don't speak their language.

They ask a lot of questions about mommy, like "When was the last time she was home?" (As if we knew, or if we would ever tell.) My sister gives us the look that says Release no information. We obey, I trust her most. More questions. Let them ask as many questions as they want because as long as I see my sister and brothers' faces, I'm happy.

We do not realize what is happening nor do we understand that this is an ending and a beginning. Then one day a new alien stands before us and says, "Come with me, we are going to find you a new home."

## Divide and Conquer

We are held captive at a spaceship called "Children's services."

If it's a service for children why do they break apart the only thing you knew your whole life –your family? It should be called adult services. They are the only ones allowed an opinion in this system.

## You Better Learn Fast Kid!

As a group home kid, I learn the ropes quickly. I don't speak the language yet, but I am a survivor so I will learn fast.

I wonder when my mom is coming back to get us because it does not cross my mind – the first few years anyway – that she could leave us with these strangers, forever!

## Adjusting to the Group Home

The first year I adjust to the other captives and see how i can protect myself from the bullies, bad kids, and people who want to touch you where they shouldn't.

We came to the group home with only a plastic bag, but some kids think there is something to steal. They test my older sister's patience.

She has none. Constantly in fights to protect you, she would later be labeled a trouble maker or too "motherly" and protective of us.

Somehow you figure it out.

For some, this is where the trauma begins.

Mother and baby brother are  gone. We are in a place unfamiliar and now we have to defend ourselves like sheep around wolves.

I am only five years old but this is where I learned not to sink but to swim.

I make a promise to myself never to be like mother and leave my children nor would I do drugs or let myself down.

Seeing your mother "nodding" out or not coming home because of drug blackouts is confusing. You think you are OK because you kept each other busy or laughing.

You have each other.

When you were home and had no food, you would sneak out to find food.

Auntie would ask you to come eat, but you knew you better not be caught because mom would be upset and remind you that you could be taken away if you go outside. Your home is your safety, too bad there was no food.

No matter what happens from here on in, I know I am special. I figure it out: I were not aborted, thrown in the garbage or (like the neighbor's kid) beaten to death by your mom and her boyfriend.

I was meant to be here and i had to find out why . . . maybe I would save a life one day!

Now i start to have my own voice.

## You're Being Shipped Out Kid

I am around 6 years old, still in a group home.

I sit with my brother Rob and sister T all day.

Only leave the room if we have to eat.

They did not want us to be together, they would do anything to separate us.

The agency still had our baby brother Mark with the same family because he was only a baby.

The social worker said he would see us every week.

They wanted us to be independent of each other, forgetting that until they came in all we depended on was each other.

The three of us get lucky and are all sent to the same foster home!

We have to leave soon. My sister walks in the room while two teenage brothers are making me play "mommy" in a game of house. They wanted to do what husbands and wives do to have babies. Thank God T came in on time!

T is mad. She tells us to pack our plastic bags and meet her on the porch. We listen. Then she is running out of the burning house telling us to keep running to the train.

There the policemen come by in a car and ask us do we have a mommy. T says, "Yes we are meeting her now." They know she is lying and pick us up. We are in trouble now.

T gets sent to a place. They think something is wrong with her but she was just protecting me from those evil boys.

Now we go back to the group home but this time T is away from us.

We see T but she is always mad and worried about us. We tell her we are fine. I will protect Rob and pray for Mark.

Every month some people come and look at us. The worker says they may want to take us home.

If you're lucky you will feel like a real family with one of your real siblings. I still have Rob. My baby brother still stays in Elmsford. (I would later find out only 13 miles away!)  Less than two years into foster care,  Mark would be adopted right from under us!  Up until his adoption we had regular weekend visits. Then one visit (the last visit) they just told us, "Say goodbye to your brother, he is young enough to forget about this [like that would make us want to give him away], the doctor's family, with a daughter, wants to adopt him."

## Mom Will Come Back?

How could mom let this happen? We have not seen her in a while. We use to see her every weekend then she started coming less and less. Now it's been months we have not seen or heard from her. She will come visit us again like she use to. We don't get to see T as much now either. I wonder if she forgot us or they made her forget us.

We must be careful not to bond because my mom is coming back as soon as she gets off of drugs. She always leaves and comes back.

She is just very sick, she will come.

The last time she came she had on her white short-sleeve knit sweater with the red, white and blue trim. I remember because it was hot and she had a bag full of chocolate candy: Baby Ruth, Charleston Chews, Hershey's, a pocketbook full of chocolate. We went down by the water and picnic tables. My favorite visit . . . my last visit with all of us!

The marks on mommy's arm were gone. Maybe she wasn't sick anymore!

Months pass.

We don't see mommy for a long time. They say she is sick again. They say they can't find her.

They say if she does not come, she will lose us.

We are not lost.

I never give up, she will come.

**Nothing Will Stop Me, Not even Abuse!**

The worker comes and takes Rob and me to another foster home.

We are excited because after two group homes, and a short stay in one home, this is our first foster home with parents and brothers and a school! Rob and I can never be separated. I am his keeper and he is the reason I still breathe. I could not forget my mom left us. Why? We were good kids. I will never leave Rob.

**A Vow to My Stolen Brother**

The last time I saw my baby brother Mark, I remember like yesterday.

It was at the end of summer, 1973. We were standing in the driveway of my foster home saying goodbye until, we all thought, the next week's visit. I was around seven. Mark was still living with the doctor's family in Elmsford, New York; Rob and I were living together and T was living in a group home. Up until then we had been visiting regularly. I don't recall a talk about finding Mark a permanent home, but how does a seven year old know even what permanent means?

It was not suppose to mean goodbye forever.

"OK say goodbye to your brother Mark, this will be the last time you see him, the family he has been placed with wants to adopt him"

We looked at the social worker like she was crazy. How could they just take our brother away forever? What is "adoption"? That word is so unfamiliar we ignore her.

"Your mommy is not coming back, we can't find her," the social worker goes on, explaining that she needed to find Mark a family while he was young and could forget. I thought we were his family. No one cares what I think. Will he forget us? I won't ever forget him. I take a picture in my mind of his golden face, freckles and reddish brown hair, and lips red like watermelon candy! No one can make me forget this picture.

We hold onto Mark so tight, my foster parents have to come out and take us apart! We don't let our baby brother go easily. The agency ripped my heart out when they took my baby brother away. We talk about Mark all the time. We wonder if he still remembers us, if he still loves us most.

Mommy still has not come back or called. The social worker says they tried to find her again but this time, if she doesn't come, we will not be hers anymore. She lost her rights. I don't know what that means; I guess it's not good.

Mommy loses her kids, kids stay in the system. We don't see T anymore. They say she is OK, just too much influence on us. I miss her. I hope they don't take Rob from me, he is all I have, the reason I breathe.

I will search for you Mark until my last breath.

## A Silent Ward

If T were here my two foster brothers would not be hurting me anymore. I can't say anything. They might hurt Rob then or the system might decide to separate us, which would kill me. I remain silent.

I am now a "ward" of the court. The foster parents wants to adopt Rob and me, but I say no because one of my abusers was adopted.

I had become a sex slave for two of my foster brothers. How could I be adopted into this family now? Brothers are not supposed to hurt you; I would never hurt my brother or anyone. Why are they doing this to me? Maybe I am ugly and stupid like they tell me all the time. Does God hate me? Did I do something bad I don't remember?

No, I think they are just evil boys.

I know I did not do anything wrong.

I can't say anything. They may hurt Rob or they may take him away from me. Quiet.

For years no one knows. One was a teen drunk, the other was a future sex offender who would serve only seven years for trying to molest a teen at the school where he worked. Because of a plea bargain deal, he never got in trouble for molesting a four year old niece-in-law, (who was living with them when she was four),  who told she had been abused when she was eleven; she saw it on a television show and realized that her uncle did those things to her.

No one believed her but me and her mom. It got swept under the rug, thanks to plea bargining. I feel disgusted, like I was his practice.

If somebody would have listened to me, if I would have only spoken of the pain with my mouth not my eyes, she would not be hurt. I feel awful.

I hope God forgives me and I pray for her everyday to be OK. I am older now. I am very angry.

This makes me sick. They never believed me and they got away with it. I would rather not have this as my family. Rob is sad, but he knows I have a reason so we will live without family, just him and me, and maybe we will find T.

## Building a Mental Wall for Protection

You let your life blur through so you won't feel the pain from the abuse. You build a wall to protect yourself.

No one knows for years.

Abusers don't think we have any rights. "You should be happy you have a home, you're ugly and stupid, nobody will want you." "Your own mother gave you away." This is what they tell me all the time. You go through life like a blind man in the dark. Blackout...

## Your Secret is Discovered

My foster parents find out what has been happening to me and so there won't be any embarrassment, they ship me to a girl's home in New York City with twenty-two other girls (just like Madeline!).

They lie to the agency and say I was experimenting with sex. They forgot to tell them it started happening when I was nine, and they also forgot to tell them about the abuser, whom they had adopted.

An Aunt from the south had surprised us with a visit. She wanted to sleep in my twin antique bed because it was closest to the door. When one of my abusers came in, she heard his threats and turned on the light. The next day she told my foster mother.

Who lied, lied and later got rid of me.

Now that she is lying, I act out. I am fifteen and mad. Three years pass.

I will have to do like my abusers said and leave my last sibling, for a girl's residence in New York City.

This place turns out to be my savior. I meet other girls who were ripped out of their homes just like me. I meet a counselor who believes in me and I find my voice and my talents so that I can escape the pain.

No one has ever believed in me. I must do well because for once somebody expects me to!

## Healing Thyself

Your barriers start to melt because you start therapy. You read all you can on the subject of what has happened to you.

You go to school to get away from the ignorance that got you here.

You learn all you can about people who abuse.

No family to trust. Can't see brother too much, he is at the enemy house.


## Love Can Heal All

I am older now. Finally at twenty-one I am legally free. A new life starts off in New York City and then, off to Paris to model.

I discover a new world!

Traveling all over Europe, I learn Life may not be so bad when you keep moving and learning new things.

One day I meet a friend who becomes my love. I have a child, life changes. The abuse doesn't matter anymore because I have life in my hands.

Life becomes clearer. Education starts. I leave my love and find another and have another life. The abusers don't exist anymore.

I have two kids and life has come full circle.

With therapy life starts to make sense.

## Illogical Logic: What did I do wrong

Now that you understand what was going on when I was a child and how I felt when I was taken away and later separated from my siblings, you can see that the first question any child might have when he is taken from his home might be – What did I do wrong?

This is the shortest chapter because you did nothing wrong.

Some say we pick our parents. Well I don't remember so I don't expect you to.

If you are alive and breathing, nothing is wrong! You are to be celebrated for being alive. Now I will show you ways to be full of life and enjoy every moment!

Don't waste time with what did I do wrong? Take on a new outlook right now. Ask: What can I do to make this work for me? How can I improve myself so that starting today I can live in this world without my family?

When you do something wrong, hold yourself accountable for it and change it. But when it comes to being in foster care, your parents are the irresponsible ones, not you!

You will find life throws all of us a curve ball every once in a while. If you are to live in this world in peace with yourself, you must learn that the bad things are only as bad as you let them be.

Focus on getting the most out of life and the most out of yourself.

You are not the only orphan in the world, the only abused person, make good out of your bad!

Your job is to turn this negative into a positive by being the best you, despite your circumstances.

Learn to laugh at difficult situations; no matter how odd or bad, find something you can learn from every situation.

My parents giving me away was a blessing in disguise because I would not have gone to good schools, met good friends, or been as stubborn to advocate for children as I am today.

You can only do wrong when you don't do anything. So what are you going to do today?


## The Environment You Knew

The home and family you once knew are gone, but hold onto the good memories. I liked to think about my sister sneaking us outside to play in the park or steal food to eat. This was our time for adventure; I did not see it as a bad thing.

I also remember thinking we were stealing chips from blind lady Helen's restaurant.

One day she pulled my sister to the side (not knowing I was listening), and told her she never had to steal, that we were always welcome to sit and have a meal at her counter. Thanks to her and the Italian store owner who let us take bread once a week, we never starved.

If they were not so kind, I might not be writing this story. It does take a village to raise a child.

Because my neighbors back in the late 60's looked out for us, social services never got called until there were no options left.

My neighbors at Rockaway Avenue looked out for us and I wish I could have said thanks for being a good neighbor.

We never worried about pedophiles or even seeing drug use. Even in the chaos of a missing mother, we were blessed.

# 3

## Oprah May Be Listening -
## Ask Questions – It's Your right!

You were born with a mind, use it or lose it! Freedom of speech is a powerful amendment to the constitution. Look it up on Google and find out why.

You are in a great country that supports children's rights; take advantage of it! In some countries, children are told to be happy they have a roof over their heads, period. There are places in the world where it's legal for families to sell children for sex.

In the United States, we have agencies that work just for children. They are making changes and really helping kids to be in a better place when they age out of the system. We have Court Appointed Special Advocates (CASA)1-877-80VOICE), an organization that advocates for children. Plus, Legal Aid is free and always available, search GOOGLE to find one in your area. These two agencies have helped thousands of children.

Thanks to these child advocates, you have rights!

If you are confused about where you're being taken, if you're not sure why you are in a certain school, if you're in a place you don't want to be or if you feel it is dangerous, SPEAK UP!

A lot of times adults assume you are going to go with the program, but if you feel your life is in jeopardy you don't have to, you're in America! Learn to take advantage of being here, even if you were dragged from Africa or tricked and cheated, like the first Americans.

 Be thankful and know you are here because people unselfishly laid down their lives for you. Your ancestors who died to get you here, slaves and  holocaust victims, did not die and be abused for nothing; show them you appreciate their sacrifice just by asking questions and challenging any thought you are told to be a part of. How do you think Hitler and slave masters got so far and killed so many? Because not enough people challenged their sick idea! No one asked questions!

Take advantage of all the agencies that will help you if you are a child. Yes, I know bad things happen while children are in foster care, but bad things happen anywhere and everywhere. Some agencies, in the Midwest say, may have more incidents of neglect by social workers because they are less closely watched by the media or less accountable than agencies in larger cities and states.

Agencies and social workers need to be on alert at all times, regardless of the zip code, color, job title or finances of a child's family.

My experience has been in New York State. As far as children's services or rights go, I believe it is one of the best states to be in. But wherever you are, you as a foster kid have rights and allies. Take advantage of them.

The girl's residence that I lived in was remodeled by Oprah! It all started with social workers, staff, and the girls who lived there asking questions about the looks of the place. Every place needs an update after twenty years; we got ours because someone asked questions!

Orphanages in other countries are low on funds and the children get neglected, sold, and taken advantage of a lot more than here. There are always going to be error in the system but if we make changes, the errors can be corrected and we can raise more powerful children.

When I look back to when I was young I realize I never asked questions, I did as I was told. I believe I learned this behavior while in foster care.

When you are placed in a home or a group home at a young age, you feel lost and you think that you have to do whatever the people in charge tell you to do. You do have to do what the agency tells you but you can ask questions and get answers today!

Remember this rule: EVERYONE HAS A BOSS, EVEN THE BOSS!

Find out the chain of command: your case worker, that case worker's supervisor, and whoever runs the whole agency. And if you find out what government agency gives your foster care agency money, you will know who their boss is.

Once you find out who is making the money and getting the money, find out which state you're in. The governor is next and keep going up the ladder. Write letters to the president and the media if you feel your questions are being ignored!

Agencies that I spoke with informed me that they have the child's best interest at heart and things have changed since the Seventies. I can tell by visits to my old group home that they have. Not only did Oprah make over the place, but they all got luggage for vacations and now all twenty-three girls go on vacation every year! This is great progress. It was embarrassing coming back to school after the summer and everyone but you had a family vacation story. Now the new girls can tell all about where they went. Now they have luggage, not a plastic bag.

If you do not ask questions, people are more likely to take advantage of you or leave you out of important decisions. When I left my foster home after my abuse was covered up, I asked a question and got an answer. What are my choices now, I asked.

I was given a list of girl's residence in NYC. I chose one in midtown because I liked that location. And I chose a place that was run by Catholic nuns because I thought it would be different from other group homes.

I was right. One difference was that our girls asked questions and did  not stop until they got an answer, and from Oprah!

Ask questions. It's your right. And guess what – it works.

# 4

## There's Nowhere Like Home -
## Group Homes vs. Foster Homes

A foster home should provide love and care. In a good foster family you will learn that love is unconditional. That means your good and your bad. You should be learning how to love again and trust through healthy family interaction.

You are likely to learn proper family structure in a foster home. You learn how you are supposed to interact with your brothers and sisters. You learn to bond with each member, appreciating each member for who she or he is. Each member should help teach you love, patience, understanding, proper anger ventilation, and what role you play in the family.

In a good home (foster or birth), each member brings value to make the family strong. You should have joyous feelings about your family when someone mentions them. A healthy family protects its members from any haters who talk about them or try to hurt them.

Some families (foster or birth) teach the wrong skills to their children, treating one child like a favorite, doting over a boy but not a girl, rewarding a child that never tells the family's "bad secrets" while treating the other children like outcasts.

Remember, many people are dysfunctional. Most use less than 50 percent of their brain, and if they have kids, adopt kids, or become foster parents they only bring that craziness to those children.

Foster homes have a lot of advantages over group homes, but pay attention, that does not mean all foster parents are good people or even functional. Foster homes are screened but anyone can pass a screening if they know what the system is looking for. You should be a master observer by now. You've seen it all. This "family" is no different; check them out like they are going to check you out. You need stability and you better learn to identify it when you see it!

In a foster home, the social worker should identify a crazy family by the first few weeks, but I am telling you, the foster kid, look for the craziness right away and if you need to get out!

## Signs of a poorly functioning family

Please note that you will be told that "all" families have problems. This is true, but you did not leave your birth home to go live with some strangers who cannot live together in peace and work out their problems with discussions or time outs.

Here are some signs of a poorly functioning family:

Yelling. In a family, it is up to the parents to teach non-violence and no-yelling from birth, and if they don't, you will hear these families yelling all the time. Yelling does not solve anything; in fact, it pisses most people off. Then name calling follows and nothing can happen now but an explosion of anger or violence.

NO ONE SHOULD EVER YELL AT YOU with rage. A parent might yell if you cursed at them or wished them dead or got violent perhaps, but for just disobeying no one should yell at you. I walk away from yellers (unless I want a confrontation). Yelling brings some mean energy that can only lead to violence, and violence is unacceptable! The only time I would hit another person is if they hit me and I was defending myself.

Remember, no one can argue and yell at themselves; they only do it when you respond.

<u>Violence</u>. Unless you are defending yourself, violence is unacceptable! You were born with a brain because it was intended that you THINK through problems or challenges not FIGHT! Go to the zoo, animals are fighters, so unless you view yourself as animal species, you should never have to fight because you can talk and think!

If someone has to hit you to get you to do what they want, you run because they do not know how to communicate. Parents should be able to talk with a child and teach them, not hit them and scare them into submission.

<u>Lack of respect.</u> If your family members have no respect for each other or for you how can you learn what it is? How your family treats you is important to how the neighbors and your friends see you. When I pick my friends I take note of family interaction. If they don't respect their family (assuming the family is generally

loving and free of abuse), then I think something is wrong with my friend or they are ungrateful – not my type of friend and I will drop them like a hot cake! Respect should be learned at a young age in a family.

Drug or alcohol use. In a healthy family, children should not be allowed to drink underage and parents should not be getting intoxicated in front of their kids. If parents are coming home yelling or smelling like alcohol after drinking, this is not good. Children are always affected by drug use and drinking in the family. You should report your foster parent if you think they are addicted to any substance or alcohol. You already have enough to deal with; you should not have to take care of this sick person. Later on in the book I will tell you why you should avoid drugs and alcohol.

Letting children see parents and/or their friends openly use drugs and alcohol is not acceptable! Remember, one of my abusers was an alcoholic. Not every drinker is an abuser, but if someone is an abuser, of any kind, drugs and alcohol only make them bolder, and children can seem easy prey.


**Advantages of Living in a Foster Family**

Develop long-term friendships. You are more likely to develop friends for life because you are in a stable environment. When my brother Rob and I were placed with a family we were excited to find out we had moved to a home on a street filled with about twenty kids! They were excited too to have two new kids to play with. They got to know me because I stayed for ten years. With the other foster homes, I never stayed long enough to get to trust the other kids, and with the group homes there were just too many of them.

At the foster home I could build friendships. I am still friends with most of the kids from that street!

Have someone to talk with. A parent should be able to give a hug or a word of encouragement when you are down or confused. My foster mother was always encouraging and loving, even when I was wrong. I got a few spankings but I know she was not abusing me, she was just from the old southern school of child rearing. [1]

Get to know and trust teachers. Building a relationship with a teacher is important. A good teacher will identify your learning style and assign your work according to your learning ability, without labeling you. If a teacher shows some interest in a child and does not treat her like she is "special," a child can start to build confidence in her learning ability.

You may have times when teachers label you. [2] Prove them wrong. Ask for help. Being in a home can help because your new parents can advocate for you if there is a problem at school.

---

[1] During Slavery and Jim Crow, it is said you had to "learn" your child right or the master would kill them if they disobeyed. But the master is no longer alive and we are not being hung on trees for disobeying anymore so the beat-your-child-to-save them theory is no longer needed.

[2] At one school, I was labeled a "slow" learner. In reality, I was a visual learner. I learned better if the teacher had something to show me. For example, learning to add by counting a stack of real pennies instead of looking at drawings of coins on a piece of paper.

Learn holiday traditions. In a family, you learn not only rules or how to live in a society, but you learn what makes your family special and unique. Your family may eat and prepare food different because of their religion or culture. You may wear your clothes less revealing or more colorful. Your hair may be short, long, braided, or you may cover your head. Your family may speak another language. There is so much to learn from each family. Learn and respect your family's cultures, values and traditions. This way you will have something to pass on to your kids.

Enjoy vacations. Vacations are taken once a year and every family member should go. Vacation is the time you and your family unwind and learn to bond, outside the routines of daily life. You should learn how to have fun with your family, doing nothing but enjoying each other in a peaceful place. Families may rent a house or hotel at the beach, in the country, in another state . . . any place other than home for a week up to a month. Only in some parts of Europe do families take a full month. (Paris use to be my favorite place because everything closed down for the month of August. Now it's different. Everyone wants to make a buck, even at the cost of ditching the family vacation.)

Attend sleep away summer camp. Camp is where I learned to ride horses, swim, play sports, camp out in the woods, fish – all sorts of activities that may lead to your future career. You meet new friends from all over the country and learn to get along with other kids, without parental supervision. If you can make it at camp, you will learn how to behave when you're out with other people and how to take care of yourself while away from your foster home. Later, this will be important for college or just going away on your own as you get older. There are rules everywhere you go. If you learn what they are and how you can have fun and follow them, you will do well in camp.

Learn about a community. Community is a part of family life. Church, Mosque or Temple; library; after school programs and sports; first job at the local McDonald's – all happen in the community. Living with a family lets you learn about one place, with its school, library, and local stores. And if you are there for a few years or more, people will get to know and remember you.

What if you are placed in a home for less than a year? That is OK. You can still get to know the local people. Who knows? You may want to come back to visit or even live one day. If you made a good impression, people will want to help you with whatever you need.

## Living in a Group Home

A group home provides basic necessities like food, clothing, shelter and health care. These may be more reliable, if lower quality, than in a poorly functioning foster home. So if a kid comes from a neglectful background, to the point even of near starvation as in my case, a group home is a great place. The government is great about feeding children! Before we were taken into custody, my brothers, sister and I were always hungry. At the group hope we had plenty of food, or more than usual anyway. That was good.

Another advantage to group homes is that you are more likely to get to stay with any siblings you may have. It is difficult to find foster homes who want to take two or more children so placement with a new family often means losing what's left of your old family.

With these two plusses come some serious minuses. Some of the disadvantages of living in a group home are:

<u>You are on your own.</u> Usually, no one gives you a hug when you're down or notices when you're going through pain. It's not that everyone who works there is uncaring. How could they care about you when there are so many other kids to worry about? I was lucky to have a counselor take interest in me, but often kids don't get the attention and personal love they need. The state should hire "parents" to run the group home like a home, not a group facility.

You have to figure everything out on your own or befriend someone very knowledgeable about that group home. Last I checked, they don't give you a list of rules. You learn them as you go.

No one is keeping track of you. Staff may know where you go after school or on weekends but they don't send someone to check on you. So if you are doing bad things no one will notice until the police, hospital, or court are involved. Or a baby is on the way.

Learning disabilities are less likely to be noticed. Because there are too many kids to deal with, staff at group homes may not notice signs of learning disabilities. Or you may be mislabeled because no one makes the time to look into your records (if your records are even available). I was labeled "slow" when in reality I had started school late.

You learn tactics not values. Chapter One told how we were taken to a group home when I was five. It was overwhelming. Kids tried to fight us or steal our food. Bullying was common. In group homes, kids learn survival tactics. It's every child for him or herself. Family values like mutual respect and honesty are not taught.

One tactic some learn is to use their bodies to get the money, nice clothes, love or respect they feel they need but cannot get from the group home. Others may use selling drugs for the same reasons or to provide for a sibling placed somewhere else and struggling.

You can survive and be happy in a foster home or group home, with or without a birth family!

The good thing about humans is we are able to adapt to any situation, including living without family. Find good friends who will help you feel family love.

You must rely on you and learn to enjoy yourself. Find peace and acceptance of the abandonment; don't feel sorry for yourself, it won't change the situation.

Planning, picking good friends, traveling and educating yourself will teach you to deal with the life you have and will make for yourself.

We can't change our birth family but we can change our life and, wherever we are, fill it with love.

## A Note About Siblings

Siblings should be kept together when possible, even if it means a group home.

I would like to see group homes changed so that all siblings can remain together in one cottage.

You can then be taught to work together like a family unit. This is much better than being split up and raised in different homes.

That can lead to never being emotionally close again. Separation can cause bitterness among siblings, especially if one went to a "nice" home and the other child went to a group home.

If you are unable to stay together, at least know where all your siblings are placed and try to see each other.

How can you know? Talk with your social worker. She should know where they are and if she does not family court should know where all the children were placed.

You may have to pry but unless they are adopted off, you should know who your siblings are and where they are.

You don't want to end up dating a sibling you never knew. It has happened! They may also have a blood type you need or know family health information you don't know. My birth grandma was later able to tell me about my family.

Try calling your siblings every day to keep communication open.

Children separated often feel scared and alone. If you received a phone call from a sibling you would at least not feel alone and abandoned. This is especially if you have younger siblings. While they may be confused, if you show regular patterns of calling, they will adjust and feel better, knowing they talked with you and you are alright.

If you can stay in touch with a family member who was good to you (not someone who is going to bring you down and treat you awful) then stay in touch.

If you happen to have a "trouble maker" sibling, love them from far. Remember, misery loves company. Even if it is family you don't need anyone else bringing you down; you are out on your own.

I knew of a girl who found her family but they were always stealing from her. She eventually realized sometimes you are better off without family.

## If You Are in an Abusive Home

I know it is not realistic to grab your siblings and go in a case of abuse, especially if your foster parent lied. But one thing you can do is let it be known—verbally and in writing— that you object to your siblings being kept in an abusive home. This way, your siblings will always remember you tried to help them and that you cared. Plus, the agency will have paperwork showing your version of what happened.

You may not be able to help them. That doesn't mean you don't care. You show you care by letting everyone know, in front of your siblings if possible, what is going on. This will be very helpful later.

I hear children who were separated all the time ask the other sibling why they left them. They did not know it was at the agency's request. They felt abandoned all over again.

When my abuse was covered up, I wish I would have written all the details to my social worker, but I was scared.

I am telling you what I learned from not telling ALL of the truth when your being hurt. It is very hard to tell your version of what happened when your foster parent is assumed to be telling the truth.

Someone should have helped me, even if I was a "hot teen," I should not have been in that home three years after they were told of the abuse!

Speak up when you get the chance, don't be afraid of change, sometimes it can save your life. And your sibling's.

## Sibling Parents

Foster care agencies and social workers must realize our older sibling is often the protector. It does not stop because we are put in a home. In my case, my older sister saved my life and was then treated like a criminal instead of a hero.

You are often labeled as kids "too motherly" or "protective." But that was the role you often played at home because your parents were getting high or not around. hat is not your fault and they need to not penalize children by separating them. Instead they should teach them that they are now safe and can be a sibling  not a "sibling parent."

Quite often before the 1980's, if there were multiple children in the home and the oldest saved the others from harm, agencies would send the oldest away to another group home or put them in another cottage or room because they felt they had too much bearing on the younger children. Can you imagine the devastation this caused?  First, separated from mom. Then your oldest sibling, who stole food for you and stopped someone from sexually abusing you, is being sent to a mental home for what you think was an act of heroism?

**5**

## Tanya Tips and Guidance for Kids in Care plus Pitfalls to Avoid like the plague!

•<u>Hold yourself to high standards!</u> If you don't expect much of yourself, no one else will. You have to set goals for yourself and honor them by working toward those goals.

Do things better than your parents! Our ancestors were beaten, raped and killed so that we could have a better life. You owe it to yourself and your ancestors to have a quality life with meaning. By setting goals and standards for yourself now, you will more likely be able to give your future kids what you did not have: stability, love, peace, and a safe home.

•<u>Expect more from yourself and less from others.</u> You are the one in charge of your life and you can set standards for yourself so that you know when you are not doing what you need to. If you don't have any standards you walk around in the dark, never finding what you need or want in your life, friends, career or your future family. Don't allow yourself to be lazy or careless when planning your life!

•<u>Don't let anyone talk you into anything you are not comfortable with.</u> One bad decision could cost you your life, someone else's life, or your freedom. Think before you act. A rule I use: if you have to contemplate doing something too much, don't do it or wait until you "feel" it is right. If it could send you to jail, an institution or the hospital, don't do it! If your reputation is at stake, don't take the chance.

•<u>Know the difference between right and wrong.</u> If you don't, ask somebody who does. Learn to speak up for yourself without violence and hatred.

- <u>Learn to control your feelings or they will dominate your life.</u> When you first come into care anger is expected, but after a while you should be releasing your anger through sports, journal writing, or therapy, not through violence. Dr. King was very angry with how people were treated during the civil rights movement, but he did not want anyone fighting because he knew that you can get more done with words and by advocating for yourself. You are a leader and leaders don't fight with their fists; they use their brain to get results.

- <u>Find a therapist you connect with</u>. It is difficult to have parents give you up. It can take years of therapy to heal. Although you have mandated treatment, I suggest you find a therapist who you connect with and can share past issues with.

- <u>Learn to read better.</u> Literacy will be your best weapon. Before I started traveling to Europe, I was already there in my mind, by reading. Find writers that interest you and make you curious to finish the story. No you don't have to read all the books on self help, but I would like you to go to a library and ask the librarian where the self help books are. You will find reading them can help you better yourself.

Any reading is better than none, so if you like comic books or novels read them, as long as you read! Reading takes you to another world and lets you get away from what is going on in your life while your eyes are on a page.

- Don't make excuses. Not having a parent is no excuse for failure actions! God and the universe supplied you with a brain to use when in doubt. If no one positive is in your life, look at all the people around you who are doing great. If what they're doing is legal, follow their ways. If no one positive is around, look at celebrities who stay out of trouble or read about ancestors who survived coming here on a slave ship without parents or family.

- Travel. Traveling teaches you about other cultures and gives you appreciation for what you have; go as far as Asia if you can. If your school is taking a trip, raise the money and go. Your eyes open to the world when you travel. When you see how other orphans are treated in other countries like India, Brazil or Russia, you will view your problems in a different way. Gratitude will appear. Traveling gives you an attitude of gratitude!

- Know that you do have options. You will not be in a group home forever. Learn all you can in school, education is your best weapon. Learn what you do best; reading writing, singing, dancing, sports, organizing. God has given you many gifts in case school is not for you. Use them, but learn what your gifts are and how to master them, they usually can bring you money.

•<u>Plan your future.</u> Plan on what you want to be in the future and figure out who you need to talk to to make it happen. Write down your goal with dates to be completed by.

•<u>Use your staff.</u> They have resources and if they don't, use the internet. Google anything you need to know. Staff knows 95% of what is going on in the group home and some of your case. Some agencies may not allow the staff to see certain information because of confidentiality laws. Staff had a life before they met you. Try to get to know them; they will help if they are able.

•<u>Talk with teachers.</u> If you look for good guidance your protector will send you someone to for answers. Learn to ask questions. What you don't know could hurt you! Teachers are very resourceful and usually like to help, if they can.

•<u>Remember that you have a higher power looking after you.</u> If you don't believe in God just know a higher power is watching over you. That is why you are still here! The universe needs you and your spirit. If you don't figure out what your purpose is here, you will stay confused. I knew when I first got raped and tried to kill myself, that I had to have a purpose or I would have died. I did not know what it was but I knew.

To help me connect to my higher power I did one exercise that anyone can understand. Close your eyes and tell yourself you're a peasant. Then do the same except tell yourself you're a queen or king. Your attitude in life is different if you know you have purpose and worth!

- <u>Don't lie.</u> All the covering up for your family and lying to social workers was NOT a bad thing. This was a survival technique you used to stay alive. You should be given an Oscar award! You will now de-program yourself and, instead of lying, tell the truth and ask for what you need. Don't manipulate other people or use other people unless you have to for survival. I want you to realize that from today on, you do not have to lie, cover up or fake for ANYONE!
- <u>Develop a strong mind.</u> Read self-help books. Listen to the DVD "The Secret" daily. This will affirm positive thoughts and teach you how to stay focused. Reading positive information helps a great deal. If you don't have people around to pick you up, do it yourself with reading.

Finally, You can do it! Like Nike's campaign states, "JUST DO IT!"

## Pitfalls to Avoid Like the Plague!

- <u>Sex (before YOU are mentally and physically ready).</u> Because of my abuse, I let a couple of guys use me before I caught on. No one told me: I am wanted more by guys if I don't do it! If your partner can't wait, dump him (or her). He only wanted you for sex anyway. A person who cares about you will wait as long as you say.

Sex is a big thing among teens now but I advise you to wait at least until you are eighteen. YOU ARE NOT MISSING WHAT YOU DON'T KNOW! Ask yourself why you really feel you have to do it now. If you cannot come up with a good answer, don't do it!

I do not condone sex before marriage or commitment before eighteen because you have not developed enough mentally. If you do have sex, always use protection. A partner may not tell you if they have HIV, AIDS, or other sexually transmitted diseases.

- <u>Pregnancy.</u> Why burden yourself with another mouth to feed? Why set yourself up for less love, because now you have to give it to your child. Love you first. You may become frustrated at the child and not be as loving as you could be, had you learned about self love and followed your dreams first. It's all about you, and then comes mate and family.

As a foster kid you don't usually know about love of self. Once you know yourself then you can venture but you do not want to end up with kids before you are ready. This has been done by me and many single mothers but I am sure if you ask them, knowing, learning about and loving self would have been a better option because when you have children, you want them to do better than you, how can you do this if you did not work on YOU?

When will you have time to talk with a therapist, you have to think of how you are going to feed your child. Being a mother means pushing all of your wants and needs to the side. Don't count on daddy to be there while you go get help, he may be with his new mate!

- Prostitution. Disease is all you can get. This profession wears out the body and the mind. You never need to sell yourself. That's why you have talent and hidden gifts that you need to learn to use. They will be your money makers.

Often victims of sexual abuse turn to this form of self-abuse of their own body. They have an "It's mine and now I am in charge," attitude. They may do this to escape pain but believe me, it is a dead end street!

Aids and Hepatitis C are major health risks, not to mention what this type of work does to your self esteem. Most prostitutes will turn to drugs to get numb before doing a job. You can see this is not a profession for you. You did not survive being abused to go to more abuse. Get another career. This one is not an option.

- Stripping for money. Same as prostitution. You don't need to exploit yourself anymore than you already have been. Remember how you felt when you walked into a new group home, all eyes on you: fresh meat! You are not a zoo animal or prized possession and don't let anyone treat you that way. They can be in awe of you because you are so great, not because of your body. There is nothing wrong with being sexy if you choose but you should not be in the sex business. You will just further exploit yourself. Don't listen to strippers who say they are happy making that money because it cannot feel nice to walk in a room and people only want to have sex with you.

What are you going to tell your future kids – I needed money so bad I had to take a chance on dying or having men touch me with filthy money? You are of greatness; this profession is not an option, guys or girls. Only people who think low of themselves would choose this career. Some in other countries may need to resort to the sex trade to feed their kids, but in the U.S. we have food pantries, churches, synagogues, food stamps. You have options besides selling your body!

- Pimping? Please! Yes, it still exists. I have meet young guys I tried to discourage from this field. They think it's OK if the girl asks them to do it and they don't hit her. Please, you have got to be kidding! Don't ever put yourself in a place where you have to get your money from another person who is doing all the work! This is the lowest profession and you are telling people you are a vulture, feeding off of and taking advantage of a dead carcass. I say this because a woman selling her body is usually a woman who has lost her soul. When you are able to sleep with strange men, at some point you had to talk with the devil for a while. At that point male or female you are a walking dead body and only vultures like pimps will feed off of you!

- <u>Bad relationships and negative people, places and things.</u> A negative person is anyone – family, counselor or friend – who wants you to participate in activities that will alter your life in a negative way.

- <u>Abusive partners.</u> Stay away. They break what little spirit you have left. Why would you be with anyone who talks to you loud or raises a hand to you? You have NOT lost your mind, but fooling with an abusive partner you will lose your spirit and your mind – literally, by being hit in the head so many times you can get brain damage. You never deserve to be hit by anyone. Don't allow it and don't put yourself around people who make you use violence. Violence is not productive and never gets any results; agreements, negotiating and talking does!

Also, you do not want to end up with partners that take advantage of you or abuse you because they know you are in the system and do not have many options. More about relationships in Chapter Six.

- <u>Gangs. The streets can't replace a mother's love so why settle. There is no love. Being "jumped in,"</u> who would beat the person they loved? Who would make you sell drugs or wear colors you may not like? Gangs are a false love that does nothing but lead you to death, jail, and in this day and age AIDS. Find good friends instead. If you want to belong to a group, join an after school sport or theater group.

- <u>Drugs and alcohol</u>. Pitfalls for anyone, especially foster kids who have no one to pick them up! You brain is just developing. How can you reach maturity if you are putting chemicals or alcohol into it? There are lots of vultures waiting for you, don't fall victim to exploiters.

When I came back to New York from modeling in Paris, as I went out each night I noticed drug dealers at famous night clubs. They did not look like street dealers; in fact, they looked like models or fabulous people.
They would often try to get me to do a line or two, but I always lied and said I already did some because I knew this was a pitfall waiting to bring me down. A few of my model friends later became addicts because of this.
When you come from a foster kid background you must avoid drugs, even marijuana, because you are already hurting and once you add drugs or excessive drinking, it all becomes a blur and you will lose control!

You will have plenty of time to drink, if you choose, when you are over twenty-one. Get your life and career together and have your home, coop or apartment.

You are in foster care; you need to be alert at all times! Getting high will not change your problems; they will only get worse because now you are ignoring them by getting high instead of talking to a friend, counselor or therapist.

Trust me: if I know nothing else, I know that talking problems out is better than numbing them!

# 6

## Tanya's Guide to Finding Good Friends and Mates

Know that you are loved and you are not desperate. I often put in my mind that I was less than the other girls because I was a foster kid. NOT TRUE! You are just as special as YOU say you are! If you don't believe it no one else will.

When you pick a mate, let him or her know you are special and you have high standards. Plan what type of partner you want to be and accept nothing less than the best in your partner.

If you have never seen normal, healthy relationships look for them on TV or in magazines. Screaming, arguing all the time, and hitting—not normal. In fact, end any date that has a lot of drama in it. You are young, beautiful and talented. Move on!

Here is my high-standards guide for picking a mate:

- Look for someone who brings out the best in you. Find a partner who really brings out the best in you. And you should do the same for your partner. Examples that I see: The late great actor Ossie Davis and Ruby Dee, Will and Jada Smith, Camille and Bill Cosby, Michelle and President Obama, Rita

Pearlman and actor Danny Devito, just to name a few.

Who knows what goes on behind close doors, but you can use anyone as a model if the relationship appears to be healthy, loving, and respectful.

- <u>Avoid drama.</u> If you fall in love young, there should be no drama: no yelling, no taking advantage of a partner. I was fortunate to live in Paris briefly enough to learn new ways of relationships. I met a young man who was loving and kind in a way I had never known, always putting me first.

Ironically, from age nineteen to twenty-one, I attracted good men. After that I attracted men with drama. I believe it was because I was traveling all over the world to escape my abuser. I was able to cover it up for awhile, so a guy looking at me only saw a happy model who loved life. As I got older the abuse was consuming my spirit and my aura attracted men who did not care much about me.

I was too young to be with a drama man, but I have since learned and I pass this on to you so you know. You are it. Live life and enjoy and don't let anyone stop your progress.

- <u>Watch for clues.</u> You will often get a clue when someone has drama and is a loser. Listen to the clues. Some obvious ones are yelling, stalking, checking your calls, lying, and hitting. Does he or she smell like alcohol or have friends who are addicts? Warning. Other clues are unreliability (don't do what they say they will do), no job, no high school diploma.

Ask any abused person and they will tell you that the jerk reveals their colors within the first month, but they were too much "in love" to see, hear or smell the clues! This applies to friendships too!  No time for fake friends or followers. You're a leader and you can always find good people.

•Be picky. When you are college age with no kids, there is always a guy or girl out there. We just usually settle for whatever comes our way, instead of rejecting them the minute we know they are trouble! Wait until the right person comes along.

• Value yourself. If you don't believe your special, no one else will. This applies to friends as well as mates. I always had high standards. My foster mother instilled them in me. I wanted friends who were smart and went to class. I figured if they cut now, what future could they have? I was right. All the friends I stayed away from in middle and high school became losers and all the ones I knew had goals, did something meaningful.

I knew a lot of famous people when I was modeling; I was not good at bonding relationships and later lost touch with most of them. I even dated a couple of rock stars (whose names I can't mention because I didn't get their permission). Let's just say if I sang one of the songs anyone over thirty would know the artist. I did not seek out rich or famous men; they came to me because I projected that I was somebody and everyone wants someone they think is important or beautiful.

Through modeling I learned that I was striking and could get attention walking down a runway and make hundreds of dollars an hour while traveling the world. What a boost for a foster girl's ego! Although that was not a lot of money in the model world, I was more than happy to make that kind of money  before the age of twenty-three.

- <u>Surround yourself with people who care about you.</u> And who want a good future for you. If they are skipping classes, missing school, smoking marijuana all day, selling drugs, not taking care of themselves, acting violent, why do you want to be around them? This is not to say avoid friendships with those less smart, but if you are hanging around ignorant, unknowledgeable kids, you will look in the mirror and see you. This is where you are tested. One of you will become like the other, good or bad.
- <u>Don't conform just to be liked.</u> Misery loves company. Especially when you have no one looking out for you. No one wants to get in trouble by themselves. Don't feel you have to do bad things to get friends or be popular. Bad things follow you and you don't need a reputation. Foster kids are already stereotyped . . . no mother, special learning problems. You don't need other people's ideas of you coming true; prove them wrong.

# 7

## Still I Rise!
## Tanya's Recipe for Avoiding Negativity

You should never harm yourself or anyone else. You were not put on this earth to hurt yourself or others. How do you know this? You were not born with a gun, knife or pills in your hand. In fact, you were not even born with hatred in your heart. You learned to be angry, but anger can consume your life.

It is a lot of work to be angry. Look at your face lines the next time you get mad. Look at how tense your body is. It is so much easier to be kind and smile or do a good deed. Don't let anyone steal your joy.

Negative can only react to a negative, so be positive and think positive and that is what will happen.

I know you're thinking then why did this happen to me? Who knows? But I do know you survived and that says a lot. You have to think of past victims who are not here with us today.

Don't let their deaths be in vain. I feel indebted (in a good way) to all of my ancestors and any person that was ever a victim in this life. I feel I owe them to be the best me and spread love to all who will listen. Yes, I do have down days but they are rare.

## The Earth After a Storm

Pity parties . . . Woe is me . . . Why me . . . I should just end it.

Stop the crap! You shouldn't ever harm yourself or feel sorry for yourself.

You are alive! I cannot express how much it means to have your mind, body and health, especially after surviving abandonment and abuse.

I have talked with victims who have lost the use of body parts and they still don't complain.

Look at anyone in a wheelchair or someone who survived being burned over 80 percent of their body. They survived, so can you!

Harming yourself is not a solution, it only ads to the energy of "poor me."

You don't want anyone feeling sorry for you. You want to rise up and be in control of what good things are going to happen.

You are loved and needed in this life so wake up and get ready to fight.

Don't lie down and die for anyone! You came through the abuse, through the storm.

It may have destroyed some things in your house or even the house, but you are not the house, you're the earth the house was sitting on. And look at history: after the Biblical great flood, after terrible earthquakes and tsunamis, the earth is always still there. It may be covered in water or debris, but it never disappears, it only takes another form.

Think of you as the earth after a storm. All else may be destroyed, but the earth remains intact. Even when it looks littered with debris or even flooded, it's still there.


## Making it is the Best Revenge

You have no right to take a life. If you were in a situation where someone was harming you and you did, you are forgiven, but don't harm someone because you want to. As a Quaker, I am not supposed to believe in any violence but my patience stops short of pedophiles.

I wanted to kill my abusers, but in the end I could not. I didn't have the power to. But there was another time, when I did have the power, and I chose not to use it.

When I was in my early twenties and working as a model, some guys attacked me in a park in New York. They tried to rape me but failed to only because they could not get my belt off. My boyfriend at the time had loaned me that belt. The attempted rapists did beat me. They were pissed because they could not remove my belt.

I ended up in the hospital, in a coma, and almost died. I lost the use of my right hand for months and couldn't model at all. I had to wear a special cast (and learn to write with my left hand). I found out after I left the hospital and went to do lineups that the guys were just "having fun" and had tried to rape another girl before me.

I had a friend who wanted to shoot my attackers. He showed me the gun he would use. When I saw it and realized that someone would die if I gave the wrong description, I told him I did not remember who had attacked me, even though one of the men was sitting right across the park from us.

In the end I could not do it myself or let anyone murder another for me. That person had tried to rape me but I still could not take a life so easily.

Revenge is letting the other person see you are doing well. Let them know the violence has not stopped your life. In the case of children, that is an area I pray to never be tested in.


## Rise Up

The sun must rise for the earth to be beautiful and you must rise from your pain to help someone else lead a peaceful and productive life. It is easy to hide under a rock or numb yourself with drugs but you, like the sun, must rise!

You were left with a heavy load but God and the universe would not have chosen anyone else because it knew they could not handle the pain. It was known that you would turn pain into a blessing for others. Your experience may give someone else life.

After a fashion show in Manhattan or when I just wanted to relax, I used to hang out at a certain bar. I was really into punk rock then but this bar hosted Rock and Roll greats like The Ramones. (I even got to hang out in the company of the late great Joey Ramone.)

Often I would see this one man, sitting alone with his drink. One night I was feeling depressed and alone. I did not want to be around my foster family anymore and my birth siblings did not really keep in touch. I felt abandoned all over again. I had had my best years in Paris because it was far from the pain and from my abuser. Although I would not have killed myself at that point, I wanted to die. I had not worked through my issues yet.

I had only spoken to this man once, except to say hi, but this night he asked me what was wrong. He told me that he has been noticing for three years the girl that always came in with a smile, even on the night when I got kicked out of my apartment. When I was homeless and my good friend had just killed himself, I was still smiling and trying to make someone happy, so I wouldn't focus on my problems

He said he could not leave without asking me why I was not smiling this night. I told him about the foster care and all that had happened to me and then he said to me with tears in his eyes,

"You remember the night I was sitting here drinking and you talked to me and told me to have faith in getting my kids back?"

"Yes," I said.

"Well I am a heroin addict, in recovery five years. I cleaned up because my wife left me and took the kids. When I talked to you that night, I had just found out that all my hard work was in vain. She did not want me to see the kids at all, and I was devastated. So I had came to the bar to get drunk, and I had bought a bag of dope that I intended on killing myself with that night. Until I talked with you and you let me see there was hope."

He looked me straight in the eye then and said, "Thank you for being alive."

That night was a turning point in my life. To save a life and not know it for years! I knew I had a purpose. This was the reason I was meant to rise above my pain. Later friends and strangers would have many stories of how I changed their lives but this was the most life changing for me and let me know, with clarity, that without me the world may be different. I just had to rise to the occasion.

You have touched people. In your hardest times, remember them, and keep rising to the occasion. Take the focus off yourself and think of how great someone is because of you. My favorite movie to show how important one positive person can be is the classic "It's a Wonderful Life."

You are always touching someone's life, rise up and be a good example for others.

## 8

## Letting the Universe Know What You Need- Homelessness is Temporary

I was homeless a few times, but I always bounced back because I knew it was up to me to find a place to live. One time, after the attack in the park, my roommate came home high off of dope and called me the N word, telling me to leave. Being that I did not want to go to my foster home, where the abuse had happened, I packed my designer clothes and went and hung out with some punk rockers.

This one girl, "L" was so kind to me. She was on the streets after running away from home because her father tried to commit her to a mental hospital when she alleged sexual abuse.

The people you meet while you are homeless, priceless.

You learn a lot by observing people in desperate situations, just how to eat and not be killed or raped that night. This is when it is crucial not to do drugs of any kind. You have to stay alert to live and get out of the situation. If people see you are just in a bad situation they may help you get off the streets.

This was my case the first time I went homeless: A nice guy and his girlfriend let me stay at their place. They knew what had happened and thought it was awful what my roommate did, especially after I had just left a hospital, no money and no job.

I learned to be kind to everyone because you never know who will be your angel.

This guy was white and had a green Mohawk and safety pins in his face as art! His girlfriend was a beautiful, thin, British black girl with a shaved head.

I had only said hello to them for years in my friend's bar so I had no connection. People use to talk about them and say they were "junkies" and strange, but I liked them for doing their own thing and, ironically, I was always defending them when someone bad mouthed them because even if it were true, addicts are people too—who am I to judge? I never told them. I just knew I liked them and they were good people.

I did not know they would be my angels. When "A" heard what happened he asked me where I was sleeping and I told him, "After I leave the bar at 4 A.M. I go to C squat." C squat was one of the worst places to crash in the 80's. You literally had to wear steel toe combat boots so you could step over dead bodies (heroin addicts who OD'd), or climb over junked cars to get to the back of this abandoned building. Point being, I was in danger!

"A" asked the owner of the bar about me and then gave me a key to his place, telling me he and his girl welcomed me to stay with them as long as I needed, and as long as I respected their home.

He was honest to admit that he was an addict, but he was also an architect who had a lovely place in Soho! I stayed with them about a month and found a job selling clothes on 8th street in the village.

I was blessed again when the owner of the clothes store put me up in a nearby hotel until my first check.

There are good people out there. Let the universe know what you need, ask for it, and wait for it to show up.

Another time I saved up $10,000 and went to California. I checked into a nice hotel and paid for two weeks in advance. As I was talking to the bellhop I realized, too late, that my pocketbook, left on the counter, was gone. A "nice" old lady took it.

It looked like, after my two pre-paid weeks were up, I might be homeless again. But I thought it would not be a problem finding a modeling or sales job. Little did I know that, at that time, Los Angeles was for blondes.

I tried finding work. I was even hired by a store on Melrose Place, only to be told soon after that the owner had changed her mind. When you're from the New York fashion industry, you get a lot of haters.

Another time, when I came back from L. A. pregnant with my oldest daughter, I stayed with my friend in the Village, and then I tried to go "home." I couldn't face it though because that is where I had been sexually abused. Instead I went to a shelter until I found an apartment.

It took a while for me to get it right because I had no one to help me, not even my boyfriend at the time. I found out he was more in love with cocaine than me.

I had no one but me, and now I was pregnant. It took a while but eventually I did find an apartment. I will say I have not been homeless since.

# 9

## If It Comes your Way
## Use It!

Even if your forty years old, it is never too late to claim your freedom. You have been through a lot, it is time to get it out and work it out of your life so that you can start living in peace.

If you need therapy, get it. If you need to go back to school to learn to read, do it. Need new friends who are supportive? Find them. The world is yours, whatever you want you can have!

For years the state dictated what you ate, where you slept, and what activities you could or could not do. Now you decide. Learn to make your own decisions. This may be hard at first but I encourage you to take a far away trip by yourself. Believe me you will learn to trust and believe in you fast!

## Take Advantage of Free Education and Services

At your age, I did not realize my potential. I was too angry with life for my mother never coming back and my being abused, and how they made it look like I was a kid who wanted to explore sex. I was never made to feel smart in school. I remember the few good teachers but the rest had barely a smile for me.

So I wasted years being angry. It took me awhile to figure out that, as a foster kid, I was eligible for financial aid and other services. You may be too. Find out. Finish school and go to college if you can.

The agency and my foster mother did not think I would even graduate from high school. I was acting out, from the abuse. But they could not understand why I was misbehaving. They expected nothing and I met their expectations.

I didn't discover my intelligence until I left foster care, went to Paris to model, and came back. Then I discovered I was not stupid or bad. I was just a visual learner who was abused and ignored and made to feel bad.

Better late than never, right?

After I became a mom, I started wondering how I could expect my child to go to college if I hadn't finished. So, when my daughter was old enough, I decided it was time to get a degree. At this point I had lived and traveled and modeled all over Europe and the U.S., gone to F.I.T for two years, had a Secretarial diploma from Berkeley college, but I wanted a Bachelor's degree and I wanted it from an Ivy league school.

I had been told I was not very bright, and I knew the psychologist the agency had employed wrote that I was not very bright (I saw the records). I did not start school until I was seven years old, so I seemed unintelligent to my case workers and some teachers. This would follow me through middle and high school. It took one good teacher to discover I was not an idiot but a visual learner. This is one reason I took so long to go back. Finally I realized I was brilliant and now I needed proof. I had a counselor help me. There are many programs for free waiting to help you, you have to ask and follow up on all leads. (And after I graduated programs like "Dress for Success" provided work clothes.)

After brushing up at community college, I won a scholarship to attend NYU full-time! Ten thousand people applied but only four were chosen. I was so proud of myself. Now I had something to pass to my daughter: knowledge.

If you are a ward of the court, education can be free. All of it. Get the good grades and talk to the right people at the university you want to go to.

Use it! Education is the best weapon in life. No one can take it from you and it helps you become a more rounded person who has an opinion.

When the job market is tight the well rounded person who wears many hats has a better chance.

When I later worked at a fashion showroom, we had our production in Europe. I was able to deal with our foreign workers when they came because I understood the culture from traveling as a model. I also worked in the music industry for a while. Some would say I was all over the place, but I would say I was where I needed to be. If you have many talents, don't let other people pigeonhole you and make you feel bad for working in different fields. I have been blessed to always find work and have peace of mind. If you have no kids, you can work two jobs and work toward a goal: a car, college, moving, etc.

## Use Social Services but Don't Let it Use You

The hard part is over, you are a survivor. The next step is working on you. Try not to fall victim to social services. We often get lead to welfare or section-8 because we have no family, but if you are young and reading this you can secure a job and save your money, use it wisely and save for a rainy day.

Always have a plan or the universe will make one for you! Make good choices that will secure your future.

Nothing is for sure but you can plan ahead.

Surviving the system means you have a plan, utilize the system and all resources!

If you have had jobs, no matter how many, and have paid taxes and all else fails and you need the system, don't feel bad.

The welfare system was designed to temporarily help citizens who work until they get back on their feet. If the country is not providing jobs and you have tried all resources, don't feel bad, it is not your fault.

While you are on services or unemployment, look for better work or go back to school if agencies will pay. It is better to be planning a future with school or a trade than to be in the same spot next year, and still have no job!

## Enjoy Life

The main thing that has come your way is your life. Use it! Hey, guess what: you are the only one that can enjoy it! Do whatever you wished to do. Travel the world, be a leader, invent something, create a piece of art. Whatever will make you happy, do it. Life is a learning journey and only you can go through whatever life brings you. The key is surviving without anger.

You should be growing and learning in all that you do and loving you while you do it. If you have to struggle with something, let it go; there are many paths, find the one that you want to travel.

Life means so much when you are enjoying the air, the trees, the water, hiking, skiing, whatever will let you enjoy this beautiful earth! You should learn to enjoy nature, it was here first. Learn the art of silence. Learn to sit in total quite for an hour, listen to what the universe wants to tell you. You can't learn by always talking or always being around the every day chaos of life. Learn to listen and trust you while living life to the fullest!

# 10
## "Get up, Get Out, and Do Something"
## Maintaining your Sanity

Your mind is all you really have left in an abuse or neglect situation. To be a survivor you must have sanity, nothing else matters without the mind. It is important to read your psychology books and if possible, study psychology in college. These classes will give you insight into what is happening to you mentally.

If you can do the work, you are sure to recover. This is not to say things will be perfect but you can cope with day to day relationships and problems.

Without the work to rebuild your mind, you may give into addictions (including food, sex and gambling). If you protect your mind, the body will endure anything.

Look at soldiers who are tortured. Another example is slavery and the holocaust; people survived these atrocities because they protected their minds.

Maintain your sanity at all cost!

No one and no situation can take over your mind, unless you let it.

Most people have weak minds because they are not trained to use the mind as a tool. You must recondition your mind by reading books like Anthony Robins' Awaken the Giant Within and The Art of Happiness by the Dali Lama.. Books like this teach you how to turn any situation around with the mind. If you go insane, it is because you allowed the evil forces to enter your mind and now you can no longer find any good to think about.

Keep your mind free of negative people. Only put in good information and positive affirmations. The mind is key to human survival in ANY situation, keep it protected. If you can stay away from TV, only watch information that will help you become a better person or better at what you want to do. TV tells you what to do through commercials, what to buy, wear, smell like, who is good to date. You should decide these things, not a TV. Don't watch unless you can understand what damage it can do.

Tell yourself something good about you everyday and if something bad happened that you cannot change, think good thoughts until you are over the situation, always protecting your mind.

I have never been an advocate for medication because it distorts the mind, making you think everything is OK when in reality, that may not be true. Your brain becomes dependent on these medications.

If you can, try to set a goal to be medication free, unless you have severe mental issues or suicidal/homicidal tendencies (you want to kill yourself or someone else). Again, therapy is better for getting through problems. Talking, understanding and processing what is wrong is the best way to maintain your sanity

**Pick yourself back up no matter how many times you fall!**

We all have bad days, but you must learn to reprogram yourself to avoid falling into depression. In fact, erase that word from your vocabulary and replace it with "I'm facing a challenge."

When I removed the word depression from my life, I found that I was never depressed again.

Doctors mean well and they do hold a lot of answers, but not all of the answers. Foster kids are more likely than other kids to be put on medicine and labeled "special needs."

A lot of times kids don't need medication. My siblings and I needed social workers and doctors who understood that we had just been traumatized from being separated from our parents and, later, each other. A little time and therapy would have solved a lot of our issues. The system will take a while to change so in the meantime, I want you to focus on you.

You can program your brain to do anything you choose, including pick yourself up after a bad event or flashback. Once you understand how the mind works, there's no way to go back. While some people do need medication due to bipolar disorder or depression, if they were willing to work through the pain, they would no longer need it. I never took antidepressants because I knew once you start, you could get hooked and then you never learn to feel the pain of what went on in your abuse or abandonment.

It is normal to feel pain after abuse, or leaving your family. It is normal to feel sick and be down. How can you get better if you don't go through the emotions and learn to control them?

One of the ways I pick myself back up is taking a long walk. Sports are a good stress reliever and so is bike riding. Do whatever it takes to get out of the funk. Your abuser or your issues win if you let them consume your life to the point where you are inactive and unsociable. "Get out, get up and do something," like Macy Gray says in her song.

## Why you are special and still standing

As I said earlier in the book, you are still here! You have meaning and purpose. You must avenge those who died because of abuse in foster care, like Lisa Steinberg. Don't let her death be in vain. Live your life and be the best you. Let that be your vengeance. Do all you can to maintain your sanity.

## Mentoring

Doing something for someone else improves your mental health. You focus on other people's problems not your own, plus helping raises your worth in your own eyes.

When I was a teenager, a girl who I knew from my middle school shared with me her experience of being molested. I use to tell her she was the most beautiful girl I ever saw.

She knew what had happened to me. She told me I inspired her to go on living when she wanted to take her own life because if I could still smile, life could go on.

Talk to other teens, you never know how your sharing will heal or help someone else.

When I worked with adolescents, a suicidal teen shared with me how she had been molested by a family member. She finally had a breakthrough because we got her the help she needed. She no longer wanted to cut herself or die.

I share my story for these reasons; I never know who is listening.

I also remember that when I was young I always latched on to what adults had to say. I remember the ones who were honest with their struggles of drug abuse or abandonment, and I also remember the ones who you knew went through something because they were so evil, but who wanted you to think they were perfect. As a kid, I saw right through them.

Share your stories, I bet someone's life will change.

## Get Up, Get Out and Travel the World

Traveling around Europe and the United States changed my life. It helped me see my own problems in a new light.

When I travel, I have a habit of going to the poorest area first. This allows me to see how the people are really living and to be grateful for whatever I have.

I saw that in some other countries, like India, China or Brazil, children have no rights and are often put into prostitution by their own family!

When I saw how desperate people were to survive and how these children could still muster a smile for a tourist, I was impressed by the human spirit.

When you take yourself out of your bad situation, you realize it could always be worse.

Traveling will teach you gratitude and humility (or you will end up being one of the hated tourists). Young people should travel every chance they get.

Don't be stuck by your current situation.

When I left the group homes I often held two jobs until the modeling picked up.

Don't be ashamed of extra work, especially if it allows you to travel and do different things in life.

## Be the Star the Universe Intended

By now you should know you are a star! Your mission is to be a light for those that cannot see.

Don't let bad things that happen in your life be your life.

Focus on all the good people you meet and all the good things that happen to you.

There is a whole world waiting for you: People waiting to meet you so that you can change their lives or they can help yours.

Many mountains waiting for you to climb them and realize their beauty so that you can tell others. Undiscovered Rivers waiting for you to throw a rock or swim.

There is someone sad waiting for you to make them happy.

Another foster child is waiting for you to be a role model. A life is waiting for you to create change.

Remember to make a plan or the universe will make one for you!

You need to be happy with you and only you. Every day think of how great you are and how much you are needed for this world to survive.

The universe knows you are a bright light waiting for all in need to see.

You don't have to be a star in Hollywood, be a star of the universe and light up the world!

# 11

## The Abuser is Always a Liar -
## Dealing with Abuse

If you were sexually, physically or mentally abused as a child, you will need therapy.

All children in foster care receive some therapy but even when you leave you should seek out a good therapist who you trust and feel safe with.

If you do not uncover your childhood issues by the time you are thirty, they will haunt you and may consume you. This may lead to drug use, sex addiction, food addiction, abuse, prostitution, violence, split personalities, depression, and suicidal or homicidal thoughts.

Seeing a qualified professional is the only way to work through these issues.

A psychologist trained in childhood sexual abuse can be a good listener to your past and will know where to guide you in the recovery process.

If they are not trained in abuse, you may not have a breakthrough for years.

I read as much as I could on the subject of child sexual abuse. I talked with other victims. Hearing their stories made me feel less isolated and I was able to share in therapy.

This is something you must share with someone so that it does not consume you.

You take back your life when you share and help others who went through the same.

Some people turn to religion but you must be careful (see below).

You don't want to end up in a cult or following a minister who is just as sinful as you. While it may help many, if you were abused by clergy, you may end up not leaning on religion, in fact hating it.

Religion will not take away your problem of being abused as a kid; it will only give you peace and self comfort when you are at your lowest.

However, if you were abused by clergy you may want to explore other alternatives. You can be spiritual and not be "religious."

Spirituality is a practice that can be felt and seen without saying a word.

Religion is what people sometimes use to control people at times or to keep themselves or others in control. It is all in how you use it.

If it works for you and helps you overcome bad things, then use it; if not, don't feel guilty: you are not "going to hell" for not believing. That is a lie they tell you in church to keep you in fear.

Only talking through the issues and working the anger will help in the long run. A lot of churches will tell you to "forget" about the past.

Being sexually abused as a child is almost impossible to "forget" (unless you develop split personalities, like Sybil or Norman Bates.

Forgetting is not a good sign.

Your abuse is the worst thing that happened in your life, but it is not the only thing.

You must find the good things and bring them to the front of your life map.

The abuse will define you but with therapy you can define yourself.

## If You are Being Abused by Someone at Church

According to some, the "devil" was an angel thrown out of heaven.

As a teen you should know that religion has helped billions of people transform their lives because the Bible teaches love. But I am no longer impressed by people who say they are religious,

I watch their actions.

If a deacon or a priest is molesting you, if a sister is beating you or punishing you in any physical way, are they really God-like?

I know of a case where a thirteen year old was being sexually harassed by the deacon of a church. The girl never told an adult. She stopped going to church, and the deacon started calling and harassing her on Sunday mornings. It took months before he stopped, and he only stopped because the girl's mother told him the girl wouldn't be going back.

I tell you this story because here is a man that all the church-goers loved. No one suspected or believed he could touch on a thirteen year old girl, especially since he was married with four kids of his own!

It was later found out that he touched a lot of the young girls at church, but he was never brought to justice because they were all too afraid of humiliation to blame him publicly. We also found out later that he was a cocaine abuser and an alcoholic who had been sexually abused as a child. Sound familiar?

This is why pedophiles and molesters get away, because victims are too traumatized and scared of embarrassment to go to court.

The only problem is, they almost always do it to others, as many as one hundred others if they are in a position of authority, like a priest.

I can bet you they are not just molesting one child.

It is a sickness and in sicknesses of this kind, there can never be just one victim.

You take a big step when you tell someone and you save a life. How many children will become addicts, commit suicide, or turn to crime or prostitution just because they were victims?

Even if you don't come forward, here are a few ideas:

- Post his/her photo in your neighborhood with a wanted sign over their head stating he/she is a pedophile
- Ride in a car and let the papers blow out the window
- Tell someone at a school or a kid who is a gossiper, just leave your name out of the story
- Call Child Protective Services

Do something so someone is aware!

Use you common sense.

Read the Bible and go to church if it will encourage positive thinking and action, but know that often people of the church are the worst sinners because they feel someone died for their sins so they can be excused from sinning.

This is a lie, and you must be leery of anyone claiming they "love God" and yet doing things not God-like. This includes all religions.

You will know if a person is God-like; their actions will always show it.

I often think of how many people professed they "loved the Lord" during slavery, the Holocaust, and the bombing of Hiroshima. Wake up!

God, as we have learned of him through the Bible, Koran or Torah, would not hurt anyone for any reason. That is why he has judgment day, isn't it?

## Mental Abuse

Mental abuse is just as devastating as physical abuse. When you are being told, as I was for years, that you are "ugly or stupid," that you will "never be anything," those are unkind words. You do not deserve to hear such abusive statements.

Never believe the words of an abuser, they always lie!

The trick is to tell yourself they are lies and let him or her think they have gotten the best of you.

In your mind during the abuse, you know you will get out and survive.

You only put up with it because you did not have many options.

Learn to put an invisible shield around your mind. Protect your mind and it will protect you from mentally becoming ill.

I saw therapist for years, but know this: I knew I was not crazy.

I just wanted to understand myself and what happened to me and this was the best way without burdening my friends with all the details of what happened.

I had friends and family gives me awful advice: "Oh that happened years ago, you should get over it."

Can you imagine how I felt, victimized again?

People may try to be comforting, but if they have been abused themselves and did not tell what makes you think they could give you good advice? Most want you to move on. I say move on too but first, know what happened and get it all out, then move on.

If you don't it will eat you alive by the time you're thirty.

If someone is mentally abusing you, you must remember, they are only words! You make them into something that can "hurt" you by believing them. Always tell yourself something good about you after someone has said something bad: I am a good person, I have a purpose. They don't have to hear you; you just need to drown out what the bad person is saying with positive thoughts and words.

The abuser is always a liar!

Build an imaginary Light force around you, and tell yourself that evil cannot hurt you because you are protected.

Tell yourself this at least five times a day
> I am special and the universe was
> made for me, I will be the best person
> I can be and live my life of greatness,
> never shortchanging or
> underestimating myself while here on
> earth. I will try everyday to be
> grateful and help others if not only
> with a smile or kind word. No one can
> hurt me mentally, unless I let them, I
> am alive!

## You Are Your Best Advocate

Tell, Tell, Tell on anyone hurting you!

Tell your social worker. If she does not remove you from the home when she leaves, call the police and social services. Do not stop until someone helps and removes you!

Here are some other actions you can take:
- Get on Facebook and Google and tell someone in authority what is happening to you.
- Keep a journal. Writing down what happened is like cleaning it out of your system.
- Learn to write letters, and then write them. Learn who is in charge of what agency.
- Call Child Protective Services (CPS). The

number is in the phone book and on-line.
- Talk to your school guidance counselor. They are trained to deal with this.
- If you life is in danger, call 911.

You are your best advocate! Once people realize they are not dealing with a dummy, they have a different respect for you. You deserve respect and peace of mind. Demand it, it is your right. You were not born in this great country for nothing. Take full advantage of being an American citizen. If you don't, you might as well go live in a country that has no children's rights. Make room for another person who really needs and wants their rights.

You are a foster child and you need adults who can be honest and help you be the best person you were meant to be. You need adult help to navigate the system, but don't let anyone use or abuse you!

You are to be true to yourself. If someone is using you, call them on it. Teachers, counselors & therapists are mandated reporters, which means if you tell, they have to investigate! Don't be scared of change; be able to stand up for yourself, even if it's uncomfortable. If you don't others may be hurt.

You do not have to be a victim ever again! I did not know one phone call could have stopped my abuse. I realize now that I should have told the therapist all of the details of my abuse, and then they would have seen I was a victim, not a willing person.

I could not tell them how one brother used to play "Cowboys and Indians" with all the kids.

You had to be captured and he would capture me and

make me do awful things.

I should have told the therapist that I was scared of dead animals because after basic threats no longer worked, one brother would place dead rodents or birds around the perimeter of the house and tell me they would make me eat them if I did not have sex with them. All of the other foster brothers and my neighbors thought I was crazy because every time I saw a dead animal, I would run and scream.

Tell every detail if you can. It will seem embarrassing at first but it is not your fault. The adults did not act responsibly.

Don't protect people that harm you mentally or physically. They will do it to other children and keep the cycle going. Be willing to step up and tell. Not only will you benefit, but others will be safer and now people will know this person is not safe.

Don't be afraid that you may "separate the family." They should have protected you. You are fighting for your sanity so do whatever you must to get out of an abusive situation! You are used to change, so don't use that as an excuse.

## If You Have Siblings in an Abusive Home With You

Try to take them or see if they will be placed elsewhere. When I was in foster care, agencies were not wise to this and I hope they know better now than to leave a child's sibling in the same home they were sexually abused in.

I believe protocol now is to remove all children when an accusation is made. When my abuse was discovered I was given an "option" to go live in another group home. All of the foster children stayed in the home, except one of the abusers, who was sent to the military.

Later I found out I was not the only one being sexually abused and my foster mother covered up the truth, stating that I was "sexually experimenting" with one of my foster brothers.

The truth is: I was told he would kill my brother, who was vey small at the time. After I no longer cared or believed the threat, it was other tactics to scare me (too horrible to mention), and finally, when I got bigger and rebellious and angry, the abuse was discovered, but I got sent away because no one believed me!

It is hard for a nine year old or a teen to come out and say someone is abusing them.

In the end the abusers words came true: I got sent away and was labeled as "bad" and the other abuser, the one they had adopted, got to stay in the home and was never exposed for what he was until years later.

## Why It's Important to Tell

Usually, if you are being abused in a home, I can almost bet, if there are other children, you are not the only one.

If there are claims of abuse or anything sexual going on, be very leery that it happened to only one child, unless they were at the home since birth and grew up as "brothers and sisters."

I am not saying this happens in most foster homes. I am saying that if one child has been abused or they are "experimenting" with a foster sibling, the social worker and agency should remove all of the children.

If you are a parent who lies to save your family name from disgrace, it may come out through that child's behavior.

If I were my social worker, the foster mother telling me she believes her two foster kids are having sex, and she wants those kids removed, would have raised a red flag to me, especially when one is years older than the other. Also, the worker should have known that with my background I was not going to say anything about any abuse.

I was sent to a group home and my brother stayed and became a problem. I felt like I let my brother down and I could no longer protect him.

There is no love in a group home setting, just counselors getting a check. Once in a while you may find a few good ones like I did but it is rare. They don't earn much and the hours are nights and weekends.

When I was at one group home the night shift always seemed to have less energy and they usually were not too kind.

You can always find one good person that will help you. Use your street smarts and your sixth sense!

If your counselors are abusing you, find someone you can trust to tell. You should not be in an unsafe place, especially if you are being abused sexually, physically or mentally.

No one—counselor, teacher, priest, family, friend, doctor, lawyer, brother, sister—no one has the right to violate you. This is America and you can take advantage of that fact. You have a right to live in peace and a right to be informed of your case.

As I said, in some countries, children have no rights. Exercise yours. People have died and suffered for you to be able to live freely.

## Have a Power Higher than Yourself

As early as five years old I knew something bigger than me was watching over me. I knew this when I heard of a child being killed by a parent or left on a step.

Later, my last foster mother was a minister. She taught me the Bible inside and out. Most important, in my eyes, she lived what she preached. She was the kind of woman I never heard a bad thing about. She always gave to others, including fostering over ten foster kids who would have stayed in group homes far worse. While I was abused in her home and she covered up what happened, I now know that she was from the old school, where things like that don't happen in my family. She was in denial.

As you get older and travel you have more understanding of other people's ignorance and almost feel sorry for them.

She was a great mother, and although she did not defend me when I needed her to, she was still a great person. Before she died, she apologized for not wanting to believe me.

Since I came to her at seven, she encouraged me to have a higher power.

While I am a Quaker, I still have my Christian based values. I don't base my life on saying I am a "religious person," I base it on doing Christian things.

## What Got Me Through It All

My knowing God was watching out for me because I was special. A higher power is a great way to protect your mind during and after chaos, and when you are at your lowest (suicidal or homicidal). This higher power will bring a feeling over you that will NOT allow you to do what you were thinking!

A higher power is like having a secret weapon. When you are looking in your abuser's eyes, or your mom has not come home and you're hungry, you have a feeling that this will pass, life will get better.

You never lose hope when you have a higher power and truly believe.

When someone commits suicide, they did not believe it would get better, there was no hope.

Having a higher power gives you hope that no one, or situation, can take you from you.

Look at people who were burned over 90 percent of their bodies and still walk around with their heads up high. Look at someone you think is barely surviving, but they muster a smile each day and never complain.

Even if they don't know it, these people have a higher power. That is the force that warms their heart when they are at their lowest, telling them the next day will be better.

## You Must Have Hope in Your Life to Navigate in this World

You are only here temporarily and, according to some, you picked this life. If you believe in past lives, get this life lesson right so that you don't have to repeat it again!

Know that pain is only temporary, the body is only temporary, but the soul and spirit live on eternally.

You should protect your spirit and soul. You can do this by having a higher power to pray to and re-charge from.

As a foster kid you often feel left out, but we have to take ownership and realize people are people. Knowing this, we need to recognize and process when we felt jilted.

It took me years to figure this part out but I did by going to therapy and talking through it.

It all works for you if you know that you are in charge of your life, not the moment of despair that you are in.

We can only be what we say we are; everything else is an illusion. Your job is to get through it and look back at it so that you can grow and be the better person.

Although I am a Quaker, I spent ten years being raised by a foster mother who was a Baptist minister.

I felt jilted sometimes by the church because they would often give scholarships to member's children going to college and baskets of items needed for the dorm, but when I graduated, they barely congratulated me.

Here I was the kid most in need in the congregation and they never acknowledged anything good I did, despite all the tithes I had paid.

Years later, after one of my abusers served time in jail, another church not only gave him an apartment to live in (with kids around), but they also helped him get a job. The church can be good, but it can also protect the evil that roams this world. Look at the Catholic priest scandal.

Overall, learning about the Bible and singing gospel became a comfort when I was going through an awful time in my life.

Without these teachings I would have turned to drugs and had a different life because I would not have thought there was light at the end of the tunnel.

My favorite quote from the bible is "I can do all things through Christ who strengthens me"

Religion is good when you use it for your needs and not man's. I like the saying never judge a book by its cover. Don't think that because someone is a priest or a minister they must be good. People sometimes abuse their power; in fact, I believe most will if given the chance and they think they will not get caught.

It is important to keep your mental focus and learn to regroup and have something to believe in besides yourself!

We all get weak, but only some can recharge the mental battery; the rest will die out mentally. Think of serial killers, murderers, horrendous people who committed horrendous acts. I think they did not have any higher power teachings or believe that there is something greater than themselves, greater and comforting.

## 12

## Reach One and Teach One:
## Tanya's Ending Message

Please don't give up when you're a foster kid; there is a message for us all. Love ourselves no matter what negative people say or what an abuser tells you, you are special. Remember, we made it against the odds and without the guidance of a parent!

Educate yourself. This is the best weapon against any odds in life. Open your mind to any book or travels that will take you out of your comfort zone. I don't want you to fall for anything, so reading and traveling is important to get a good rounded look at people, places and ideas. Accept the fact that you will enjoy life more when you open your mind and heart and try not to base your opinion on one thing you learned.

Become free of the system by setting up your future with goals.

I cannot say it enough: If you don't make a plan for the future, the universe will make one for you, and you may not like it!

Think of what you want, write it down on paper, and make it happen by talking to people you think can help you achieve those goals.

Don't tell everyone if your goal is far out (you want to be an astronaut or a TV star). People are sometimes jealous when they can't think that big so they may condemn you or tease you. If they do, remind yourself that nothing is wrong with you or your goals; the teasers are just weak minded and have no hope. Don't get mad at them.

Let your anger fuel your passion to try harder inside, never stopping until you achieve your goal.

The system is set up so that you always need some services because you don't have other resources, but you don't have to stay dependent if you plan and utilize those services: school, guidance counselors, section 8, Department of Social Services, financial aid, therapy, rehabilitation, etc.

Along with available services, good friends are a great resource. Learn to pick people who will care about you like family. Surround yourself with people wiser than yourself who love life and learning.

Get an internship and a mentor as soon as you can; they can lead you to success.

Keep a bank account or a stash of emergency money. Even if you're a great worker, times may be slow and you'll lose a job. Your stash will help you avoid desperate moves such as taking a job you hate, selling yourself to eat, living with someone you know is abusive, or putting up with people that are not good for you.

Remember you always pay to play, so if you do dirt, dirt will come and collect! There is no "easy" road to success. Only honesty, integrity and hard work.

Spend your time and money wisely; don't do careless, meaningless things that could change your goals  (gangs, selling drugs, smoking, abusive partners, buying clothes you cannot afford yet or could but should have used the money to put away for college or trade school).

You only get one life. If you abuse yourself and do not learn to enjoy your self and your life, you may not get a second chance. Look at adults who are in jail for life because they killed someone in a fight as a teen.

Value your life, time and ancestors. Many died so that you could live. Now it's up to you to have what you want.

While life in a foster or group home is hard, know that as you have breath, God and the universe are watching over you.

It is up to you to hold on and be the best you can be. I wanted to give up many times but I knew God and the universe had a bigger plan.

I knew this because I always had someone reaching out a hand to help me when I felt I was sinking.

I also prayed a lot that the universe would guide me and let me always do what is right, not what is easy.

## Your Worth

Do you know what you are worth? Are you a good person, a good worker or friend that is irreplaceable? Find out.

Think of all you do for others, how you treat people, how much you are valued, your skills that no one else has. All these traits add to your worth.

I am not only talking about a job, I mean in life! I give out a certain energy and that is usually what I get back. Good, positive energy has no price value. You cannot buy it but it is most valuable in this life. Good energy will pick you up when you're down or make lemons into lemonade.

If you have good energy don't let anyone take it away. Even in bad times, hold onto it like a precious jewel; it is the key to a good life!

Everyone needs a pick-me-up and people will seek you out when they are down or need a good vibe.

You can use good energy to get anything you want in life.

Just write down what you want or who you want in your life, be positive, surrounding yourself only with good and watch life change!

Look at your life and ask: am I getting what I want? If you are not, get to work. You can change anything in an instant, with your mind. You are worth all the earth has to offer.

## Be a Leader

Don't follow anyone. There are times when you have to learn from someone but you don't need to follow. It may lead down the wrong path.

If you have to follow, make sure the leader is at the top of their game and has something you are trying to get with hard work, goal and effort.

When I was learning the modeling trade, I had to ask girls about contracts and expectations.

I only asked girls who I knew would be famous or were making more money than me and had booked big designers like Yves Saint Laurent or Givenchy.

I would not ask advice from a girl who just got to Paris. She could not speak French and she did not know how to get around.

Be a leader. You have survived being taken away or your parents giving you away. What could be worse? You are strong if you survived this far. Why follow when you can lead? Don't you get it?

If death has not caught up to you by now, you were meant to be here! You are an original, not a carbon copy! God made only one of you. No one can be you or do what you do.

I never liked following anyone or being submissive for that matter, so when my friends tell me about an event they tell me as information not as a demand to go with them.

Decide what is right for you and don't let anyone stop you from taking action.

We all have a mind, not many use it. You can by reading and educating yourself on any topic you choose. Following others can get you time in jail and a bad reputation. And it can make more people dislike you. If you are not a leader then learn from a person that is at the top of their field and has a great reputation.

## Enjoy life

You are not your mother on drugs or your abusive father. You are unique and special and you will be different because you value life and want a high quality life. Modeling allowed me to travel and enjoy food and people from other cultures.

I did not sit in a youth hostel all day or rely on my agent for fun. I took boat rides, hiked mountains and went to museums.

Really enjoy the life you are in. Don't let it pass you by. The world has so many hidden treasures, you need to discover them.

Don't be afraid to travel alone. The first time I went to Paris, I went alone. This way I was pushed to meet a variety of people and to learn to rely on myself after years of relying on a system.

I learned to make decisions without anyone's help.

You lived through group homes and foster homes, traveling on your own will be a breeze because you already have common sense and you are a master at spotting bad situations, this is the time to test yourself!

I came back to NY, (a few times), because I was scared of leaving my brother, and being alone, hello, I was already alone!  I should have stayed in Paris, I always felt at home, even before I knew the language. Never be scared to try a new place to live, the universe always takes care of you if you follow your heart.


## Help Others

Other kids can learn from your experience in foster care. Write a journal or blog, or just share when you are given a chance. Don't be ashamed: none of this is your fault. You are making lemonade out of lemons.

Your job is to not give up, to educate yourself, surround yourself with loving people, and open your heart to help others in need. God gave us instinct for a reason. Use it or lose it. That inner thing that tells you to do or not to do something is your inner Light; if you sit in silence and listen it will lead you right.

Follow your instinct; it will get stronger the more you use it. So many people made decisions for you all of your life. It is time to hear your own voice.

You are loved and you are special!

Teach one, Reach one and they will go out and save the world!

You never know who is watching you and using you as a role model.

Thanks to all of the social workers and foster parents who work hard to help children every day.

For advice especially for you, see the Appendix.

I will end with a saying I came up with after thinking of the many adults who smiled at me as a child: "Be kind to someone today, smile, it may save or change a person's life, especially a kid."

From Tanya, who's life has been changed thanks to the village.

# Appendix

## Advice to Those Who Work with Foster Kids

This last chapter is for those who work with foster kids. Of course, anyone can read it but it is meant specifically for Child Protective Services (CPS) staff, social workers, police officers, doctors, child advocates/ lawyers, foster parents, and foster siblings.

Goals I want you to think about:

> ➤ Preserving a child's past
> ➤ Letting the child share her story without judgment
> ➤ Follow up on abuse allegations after removing the child

When CPS is called they must act on a tip of child abandonment, neglect or abuse. When you investigate a home the clues are usually all there. If a child is bruised, sad, unusually thin, not speaking, unclean with odor, malnourished or does not seem right, follow your clues and your instincts.

I know there are confidentiality laws but, if possible, interview the neighbors or family. This should be done by detectives because they have a better understanding of body language, lying or inconsistencies in a story. I know this would be costly, but you can pay now or pay when the child takes it out on society. Perhaps CPS could have an in-house detective who deals only with abuse and neglect investigations.

When CPS takes a child from his or her home, detective work starts at that moment. If not, the child loses his or her past, instantly and permanently. When children start telling stories of the old "apartment in Brooklyn," the "blue curtains in the kitchen" or "Uncle Joey," they may be called liars because no one ever bothered to verify basic family information. The social worker may tell the foster parent that the child has a "vivid imagination."

I was fortunate to see my birth grandma before she passed and she verified every story I had ever told my foster family, who at times thought I was lying. Of course everyone was apologetic, but why embarrass a child who knows the story because they were there. Even if they never see the family again, everyone wants to know his past!

CPS workers have to have more than a degree; instincts can save a child's life and keep together a deserving family that simply needed intervention services.

## Preserving the Child's Past

You can help a child preserve the past by listening to and believing her memories, and by helping them find lost family.

Listen to stories about home. A child is piecing together his past, believe him; you can always verify stories with a trusted family member. Often kids are told not to "lie" about past events or descriptions of their old home. Sometimes that is all they remember. Compliment them on such an impeccable memory.

I once told my foster family that my siblings and I had been held hostage at gunpoint by the mob. They didn't believe me. I was barely five when it happened but I actually had it mostly right, a fact that was confirmed years later by my grandma, who had been there. My mother's heroin-addict boyfriend had stolen money she made selling drugs, which brought the mob down on us, with my "uncle Luigi," someone's ex- boyfriend from Italy, saving the day by getting the money back.

No one ever gave me credit for my memory. Your memory is all you have in foster care. I was sure to keep stored my most precious memories before I went into care. My favorite two were from when my grandma made gumbo and when we visited my aunts Cherry, Rose, and Sara. Because we were always hungry and they always had food on the stove, these were my favorite memories. My birth mom had nine siblings, but these three I never forgot. I found out later the others (except S, L and Y), were on drugs or drinking heavy; that is why they did not take us.

Help them find lost family. It is scary for children to know that their siblings may be living nearby and won't be recognizable because they have not seen them since they were four years old. If you can arrange for them to meet, please do. It may help the foster child to know another sibling is alive and well and it could put closure to the "someone looks like me" feeling in an adoption case. It's no fun wondering if the person next door who looks a little like you is actually related.

## Foster Mother

Mother is the biggest job you can have in this life. You are working with someone who was given away or taken away from the only love they knew, no matter how sick it was. You are in the healing business so you should NOT take any kids if you do not have patience, unconditional love, non-judgmental skills, and a comforting spirit.

If you are taking a kid only for money, please don't. Not only will they know it, but they will make you work for every dollar! I have had numerous kids tell me they knew they were only in their foster home for money and they acted out on purpose. It is not a good feeling knowing someone is only helping you because they are getting paid. We know the money is incentive, but if you take a child, let it be because you think you can improve her human potential and give her the tools she needs after leaving foster care, hopefully becoming a great human being who is good to others.

Do not try to underestimate foster children. They are masters at identifying bad intent people. Imagine being placed in many different group homes. You deal with hundreds of people on a daily basis. You intuitively learn who is real and who is not.

Foster children are the smartest because, in order to survive, they have developed street smarts (when you meet someone and you know they are bad before anyone else notices it). Plus, they unknowingly use their sixth sense. They will not tell you they know you are in it only for money; they may just play the game to get what they want.

Remember, foster kids are used to being moved, so this is just another move for them.

You will not get respect from a child who feels they are being used.

My foster mother was a great mother. She was from the old school and really wanted to help make a child's life better. Yes, I was sexually abused in her house but I knew she had no idea what was going on because she was busy running a few businesses, assisting in the church, and raising children no one else wanted.

I still believe if I had not been with her, my life would not have been as full. My birth mother lived in Brooklyn, New York. I was able to appreciate the fact that my new environment, even with abuse, allowed me privileges I would not have had at my birth home. I know I would not have attended private schools or the best public schools in the United States.

My foster mother taught me to always have a job, or two. I owe a lot to my foster mom. Without her, I would not have reached my fullest potential. We talked later about the abuse and we understood all that had happened. She, like my abusers, was able to apologize. I was lucky to get not one but three apologies; it helped me move forward with my life.

## A Note About Lying

Because foster children usually came from homes with addicted parents or abusive parents, they are masters at telling you what you want to hear. They had to make up lies to the teacher about the black eye or convince the social worker that they were not being sexually abused because they were afraid for their lives.

Teach them to use this "creative lying skill" to get out of peer pressure instead or to get away from negative peers! When I got to high school there were some kids who got high all day. I knew I wanted no part of it! I would lie and say I was allergic, and when I modeled I would say I had already had some. We don't have to lie to anyone, but there are times when teens are caught in a trap and cannot say no. Those who can't say no need help learning what to say instead so that you don't join in something they know is trouble. You have to teach them to turn their survival skills instincts into something that can help them choose wise friends.

Telling a lie is seen as bad, but you should look at it from their perspective. They used lying to make it through the abuse or abandonment. Once a child is in a safe and nurturing environment, they can be taught to deprogram: the truth is now OK.

Therapy is an important as part of deprogramming. A good therapist will show the child he is safe and can now work with truth and reality because no one will punish him for it. I had over twenty years of therapy (5-18 mandatory if in foster care).

I went through many therapists but one in particular helped me break through my past. It took over thirty years! It is never too late but why wait, start teaching a child as soon as she comes into your home. I have mentioned therapy throughout the book because it is vital for a foster child's healing and success.

If you have a child in care who is lying and stealing, her behavior may also be a product of previous foster placements. Just because a child gets placed does not mean it was any better than the paternal home; sometimes it is worse. I was molested in a foster home and was picked on before that in a group home. I have heard plenty of stories of abuse while in the system.

At the "chaotic and dysfunctional" birth family home, the child at least has the boundaries they created: dad is drunk, mom never comes home, my uncle is abusing me, and we have no food. In the "unsafe" home, at least they can see all the evil players and make provisions: steal food; build mental walls to physically protect themselves during sexual or physical abuse; lie. In the new "safe" place, however, they don't know who the snake will be, they find out as they go. Eventually, if a child is placed in enough homes, she becomes an expert on people and erects a defense before they even enter their domain. As adults, these children tend not to have many friends and because of all the moving they are able to drop friends at any moment. They need to be taught how to trust again. Only then will they be willing to let go of one of their best survival tools, lying.

## Social Workers

The social worker is temporarily taking the role of mother. He or she will make observations that result in life-changing decisions for the child.

In a way, you are like a mother while the child is off at boarding school. The child's parent has "sent them off ," to a place where they are supposes to learn and grow. If you are not aware and ahead of the child's needs, it could turn out disastrous and the child could end up hating you. You report back to the agencies. A worker interacts with the foster parents or group home staff and the child; you should have monthly team meetings with all involved or check in and see what the child needs or how they are doing.

This child should have a team that helps plan his or her future. The team should consist of a mentor, education follow through, therapeutic needs, and activities that will prevent idle time (music, theater, sports, drawing).

When a child becomes your client you are given case history, but nothing is better than talking to all involved, if possible.

When the child is confiscated from the home you should not leave the home without doing a quick information assessment. This should include but not be limited to looking for a photo of the child.

Again, this is often the only chance for them to later see themselves as a child and preserve a piece of their history.

**Things to bring to a home when removing a child.**

- **Food**. In our case, it would have been nice to have a piece of food handy. We were starving!
- **A suitcase**. When I was being moved to group homes, I often traveled with a plastic bag; I had no "luggage." It would be nice for the worker to bring a small suitcase. Even if the plastic is for lice prevention, having one handy saves a little embarrassment for the older children.
- **A disposable camera.** A photo of the child and siblings should be taken once you're inside and it is determined they must be removed. If nothing else the child will have a photo from when he or she was younger. This may be the only photo of their siblings. I have none of my family, especially my baby brother; it may have been useful in finding him with a photo using age progression. It also may be a comfort seeing a familiar face in a picture when you arrive at a new place. When you arrive at group or foster home, you are treated different if you have no family; at least having a photo will make a child feel safe or hopeful for a future reunion.

It should be a crime to not let siblings know of each other if they were together for more than four years. I can remember back that far!

Try to advocate for the child's best interest, not just the system's.

Medical records should be obtained for future illness identification. All efforts should be made to know the child's medical history. I believe the court can serve a warrant for arrest; they should have a warrant when taking a child from his/her home. Birth records should be obtained through the court as soon as the child is confiscated from home. Nothing is worse than your doctor asking you as an adult about family history and you have no idea.

The goal for agencies working with foster children should be to empower the child to grow into a healthy adult. This is hard without knowing your basic health and family information.

If you ask, you can usually find a family member who can give a little summary: how many aunts and uncles, where the child was born, what drugs the mother or father were on, and family medical history (cancer, heart, lupus, thyroid, bipolar etc.).

I find that grandparents know more than most but if no one else is around even a neighbor or friend of the family may know something. You should not leave that house without some memory for the child. The court can get a warrant. They can get records and confiscate a child, and they should be able to obtain records.

## Doctors

Instinct can be just as important as a Medical license. They teach this in medical school but I have witnessed emergency room situations where a child is not viewed as abused simply because the parents are from a rich zip code or arrived in a Mercedes.

In the case of Lisa Steinberg, did no doctor notice her condition? No one noticed that even in her photo she looked deeply unhappy? When you first see a foster child, they're physical and emotional state should be noted.

A child should be monitored for at least 3-6 months before a decision is made to give them medications that can cause other problems. When a foster parent or social worker tells you a child is "hyper" and needs medication, they should be monitored and then given medication if absolutely needed.

I have worked with kids who were labeled and put on medication some could have lived without.

If I were a doctor and a parent told me their child wanted to hurt them or wanted to kill themselves—and the child was seven—I would be curious to find out why. Something is wrong with this family or something has happened to this child that they are not able to process or tell anyone.

We are creating  future addicts by not training youth how to deal with there "excess" energy instead of medicating them. Foster kids are becoming targets for Medications, just for having excessive energy. Please help stop this new fad, as it is huring our children.

I have always been hyper but my foster mother was brilliant—she kept me busy with singing, dancing, ballet, swimming, girl scouts, anything that would take up energy and allow me to express myself and release the energy.

You are trained to look for bruising, swelling, the same excuse for repeated black eyes, but you are the leading authority and perhaps should also look for an alternative to medication.

In the end, your decision to put a child on medication, report a parent, or suggest an after school sport may change or even save a life.

## The Court System

I am thankful to all of those in the courts who have changed children's lives for the better and still work to do so. I tell my story in hopes that a judge or lawmaker will be inspired to change some of the outdated laws regarding foster children.

**A few suggestions to consider:**

• Perhaps those who age out of foster care could be given top priority on a section-8 list.

• In addition, laws could allow them free community college until age twenty-five. Perhaps a program like work study or AmeriCorps could be developed just for ex-foster kids.

• Another idea to consider is mandatory bank accounts for kids in care, starting when they enter the system. This would increase the chance of them having money on the day they leave, not just carfare and $50. There is a similar practice for child actors. It's an account set up so no one can touch the money until they are of a certain age.

I give this advice in hopes that you will put yourself into a foster child's shoes.

With positive influence and guidance, foster children can become key people in our society and give back. You can make a difference before you see the same child as a criminal.

The judge often decides the child's fate based on what

the advocate, social worker and police reports state. When a child is old enough, if they are of sound mind, you should also ask their opinion.

## Working with Victims of Sexual Abuse

If sexual abuse allegations are made they should be thoroughly investigated. Children rarely lie about sexual abuse. They will "lie" by not telling it's happening, to protect the abuser, prevent break-up of the family, protect themselves or family members; but if they make the accusation, it is rare that they are lying.

First, no one wants to shame themselves with this horrible act. So if they say someone is sexually abusing them, even if it is not physically proven, they should be removed and asked what contact they want with the accuser (if it is a parent or sibling).

Most important for sexual abuse victims: a child should not be associating with anyone who sexually abused them. A human spirit cannot thrive with someone who virtually sucked the life out of them.

You are asking for trouble by keeping a child in the home of an abuser. Ask your local pedophile or rapist serial killer, or just ask Jane Doe who smokes crack all day and prostitutes to escape the pain, or ask me, who was molested by two of my foster brothers for years .

It was dreadful to sit at holiday dinners or to be in the same house.

I was relieved when I was sent away to a girl's

residence in new York City. I was finally away from the chaos and could now start to heal, without shame or fear of my abuser "getting" me.

I felt that my other sibling should have been removed from the home. Instead they did just what my abuser had said they would: believe him over me and separate me from my brother.

I was sad to leave but glad to be out of that situation. I did not see my brother much because I did not want to go back to that home, so they had to come to the city to see me, and I regret not keeping in touch more.

Because my foster mother lied, one of my abusers hurt more girls before he was caught. An abuser must always be stopped so that they cannot hurt other children.

I believe a person can work through sexual, mental or physical abuse if they have intervention, therapy, and no contact with the abuser.

In addition, the abuse must be told about before the child builds a cement mental wall that turns into schizophrenia or irreversible behavior.

Both of my abusers were allegedly abused while in foster care.

One was killed in his twenties and had become an alcoholic; the other was sentenced to seven years in prison for molesting a fifteen year old and his four year old niece. Remember, he did no time for molesting his four year old niece-in-law, because of his plea bargain deal!

The cycle never ends, and it is imperative that the CPS worker, social worker and therapist do a thorough job. Everyone involved in the case and all agencies can make a huge difference for the sexually abused child. In the end, we all can make a difference in the life of a foster child!